Travel

WITH YOUR Baby

Fodor'sfyi

Fodor's Travel Publications
New York • Toronto • London • Sydney • Auckland
www.fodors.com

Travel with Your Baby

Editors: Karen Cure, William Travis

Managing Editors: Lisa DiMona, Robin Dellabough, Karen Watts

Editorial Contributors: Alan Reder, Merri Rosenberg

Production/Manufacturing: Publications Development Company of Texas

Cover Design: Guido Caroti

Cover Photo: PhotoDisc

Interior Design: Lisa Sloane

A Lark Production

Copyright © 2001 by Fodors LLC

Fodor's is a registered trademark of Random House, Inc.

ISBN 0-676-90134-4

ISSN 1533-1563

Important Tip

Use good judgment and common sense in evaluating your child's symptoms to diagnose and treat any illnesses. Read all labels and seek medical advice if there's any indication of emergency or confusion. Medical professionals are your best resource in crisis situations. The advice and recommendations here are not intended to replace the advice of your physician.

Special Sales

Fodor's Travel Publications are available at special discounts for bulk purchases for sales promotions or premiums. Special editions, including personalized covers, excerpts of existing guides, and corporate imprints, can be created in large quantities for special needs. For more information, contact your local bookseller or write to Special Markets, Fodor's Travel Publications, 280 Park Avenue, New York, NY 10017. Inquiries from Canada should be directed to your local Canadian bookseller or sent to Random House of Canada, Ltd., Marketing Department, 2775 Matheson Boulevard East, Mississauga, Ontario L4W 4P7. Inquiries from the United Kingdom should be sent to Fodor's Travel Publications, 20 Vauxhall Bridge Road, London SW1V 2SA, England.

Printed in the United States of America

10 9 8 7 6 5 4 3 2 1

Contents

Have Children, Will Travel

WHERE WOULD YOU LIKE TO GO on your next trip? France, Italy, Japan, China, New York? Especially if you're a first-time parent, you may be apprehensive about taking your baby to far-flung destinations. You may even think that your traveling days are behind you. Truth to tell, though, you can go almost anywhere with your kids that you might go without them, no matter what their age. Yes, your trip will be different than if it were just you and your spouse. Yes, you do have to haul more stuff. Even preschoolers big enough for a backpack may not be able to tote as much as they want to take with them.

But there are payoffs. Few experiences in life can compare to taking your child to a familiar, much loved place, and literally seeing it again through her eyes. Or journeying to a new destination and discovering unexpected pleasures because your child has noticed something that you yourself would have missed. Young children don't require great works of art and man-made diversions to amaze and delight them; day in and day out, they find comparable wonder in the ordinary things at every turn, and when you're at their side, you will, too. You simply cannot breeze through a destination—a three-cities-in-four-days trip, not missing a single tourist attraction in your path, just doesn't cut it with most kids. Repeated packing and unpacking and a stream of unfamiliar environments throws them out of whack. So does constant rushing around. Instead, your kids want to stop to smell the flowers, literally and figuratively, and when you join them, you'll absorb the texture and rhythms of your destination as they do, experiencing it in greater depth than many a childless traveler (or the traveler shadowed by teenagers that your baby will become before you know it). The slower pace adds up to a more restful vacation. And often, as you stand sentry at a playground or follow your wobbling toddler down a hotel hallway, you will make the acquaintance of other parents, both fellow visitors and locals, and learn about the challenges and issues they face raising children in their home town.

Traveling with kids can bring out the best in you as well. Being a parent is always tough; being a parent on the road demands that you rise to another level, being insightful, resourceful, creative, and resilient. Unlike the travelers who accept the received wisdom about what they should do and see when they travel, a parent has to focus on what you and your children will really like. You learn to think about what truly gives you pleasure and what truly fires your youngsters' imaginations rather than what's supposed to do that. In the process they come into sharper focus as individuals. Then, having planned your days with your own family's interests in mind, you may end up taking in rewarding sights and attractions that you might have missed if it were just the two of you.

Moreover, if something goes amiss, you have to put on your bravest face and deal with it cheerfully, creatively, resourcefully, and immediately, because your children are depending on you.

Not the least meaningful, when traveling as a family, is the simple fact that it's a pleasure to spend time with those little people you love so well—your children—and that it's the sum of these days and hours together that creates the shared memories that are such an essential part of what makes a family *your* family.

Bottom line? Traveling with children under five is just wonderful. Like parenting itself.

CHANGING CHALLENGES

Every age has its distinctive pleasures and challenges.

Of all children under five, infants may be the easiest to travel with. Granted, they do need equipment—car seats and portable cribs, strollers, diapers and wipes, pacifiers and bottles, ointments and creams, special soaps and shampoos, and even special towels. On the other hand, babies are small and portable, they don't argue with you about where you're going, they can sleep anywhere, and—if nursing—they don't even need special food. In short, babyhood is a fine time for you and your spouse to take a family vacation, even if you're stopping at different hotels every few days.

Toddlerhood is an in-between stage for small children as travelers. Although toddlers often do fine on trips, you yourself need to do more adapting than you do for either babies or preschoolers. Enthralled and excited by the world, your little one is a pleasure to be with as he absorbs new impressions and experiences in a whirl-wind of motion. But simply keeping up with him is a challenge, and he needs regular rest in a safe and comforting place to replenish his energy. You need to build a regular naptime into the daily schedule and preserve his familiar routines. Travel is all about change, but too much can make him miserable; you need to strike just the right balance. Stay-put vacations, where you base yourself at one lodging place and perhaps make the occasional day trip, work well. So do nature destinations like beaches, parks, zoos, aquariums, and botanical gardens, where there's plenty of space to run around.

By preschool years, many of the challenges of the toddler stage disappear. Your child is liberated from diapers and toilet training and is eager to experience the world with you. It's even easier to find activities that you'll both enjoy—you can take in museums as well as the places he liked as a toddler. This is a great time for family travel—take advantage of it.

Whatever the age, having a trip that's as rich in wonderful memories as a trip can be lies in making canny choices from the outset and planning carefully for all eventualities, so that the resources you need are at your fingertips when the situation calls for them. Flexibility is key. And never try to rush—allow extra time at every stage of the trip.

In making your arrangements, keep in mind that you aren't the first family to travel together. There's a whole world out there of travel agents, hotels, cruise lines, resorts, museums, restaurants, shopping malls—you name it—who understand your challenge and have the know-how and the facilities to help you make it smooth sailing.

It's up to you to cut yourself loose from your workaday mind-set so that you can get the most out of every minute of a trip with your kids—and make it one of the high points of your journey through life together.

Planning a Family Vacation

WHETHER TRAVELING WITH BABIES and young children is exhilarating or exhausting, thrilling or terrifying depends in large part on your attitude—and your preparation. Partly that preparation is mental: You need to refine your expectations so that you don't envision something that could never come to pass. A handful of tried-and-true good-parenting techniques are just as important on the road as they are at home. Finally, you need to choose a destination that works for you as a family, with something for everyone to enjoy. Zeroing in on the perfect spot and setting all the plans in motion is the first challenge for a family traveler.

From one age to the next, any given travel destination has a different appeal for a little kid. For a couple of years, your child might focus on playgrounds no matter where you take her. Then, just as you've perfected your ability to locate the best ones, they'll interest her only marginally and it's, say, shopping that's most interesting. One year at the beach, they're frightened by the surf and want to splash around only in the nearby ponds; before you know it, they want boogie boards and love getting pounded by big waves. One year, they're just learning to step into a pair of skis; the next, they're schussbooming down a hill looking to catch some air as they ski over bumps. Or so it seems, anyway.

This changing mindscape is a challenge when it comes to planning trips for a family. But in a way, traveling with youngsters is a little like traveling with anyone else: You have to consider your companions' interests as well as your own. Practically speaking, that means picking a destination that can be appreciated at many different levels, one where your toddler can get excited about, say, the museum's colorful floor tiles, the ants along the trail, or the restaurant's novel bathrooms while you admire the exhibits, the woodlands' grandeur, or the view over the harbor from your table. You also want a destination with at least one attraction that will be really special to at least one member of the family—yourself included.

As you're scoping out places, take into account the type of child you have: easy-going or fussy? Outgoing or quiet? Adventurous or timid? Interested in rocks and flowers or music and art? Then consider what type of vacation would most satisfy you and your spouse. Do you want sun, sand, and surf? Hikes in the woods and nights under moonlit skies? Or a big city full of museums, zoos, and parks? Around-the-clock togetherness? If you already spend 24 hours a day with your children, perhaps you want to look for a resort with lots of kids' programs.

Whatever your choice, make sure that the places you choose to stay do welcome families so you don't feel as if you have to apologize for your children when they're just acting their age.

This chapter details how a handful of classic American vacation ideas work for infants, toddlers, and preschoolers, together with some pointers to bear in mind as you make your plans for your next trip—long vacations and weekend jaunts alike.

10 GREAT FAMILY VACATION DESTINATIONS

BAR HARBOR AND ACADIA NATIONAL PARK, MAINE. Acadia itself has everything from boating on quiet lakes to beaches, and from gentle hikes along scenic wooded trails to nature programs. Bar Harbor is compact, with child-friendly restaurants, hotels, and attractions.

CAPE COD, MASSACHUSETTS. The beaches facing Cape Cod Bay on the north and west of Cape Cod are great for small children. The surf is quiet and when the tide goes out you can walk so far toward the horizon that you can barely see the shore; the sandy bottom is full of tiny sea creatures. Here are also many sandy-bottom freshwater ponds, a great bike trail (and an abundance of rental single and tandem bikes and kiddie carts), plus nature tours designed for families, whale-watching trips, and lots of rental houses. When it rains, there are galleries, stores, and museums to explore. Wellfleet is home to one of the country's last remaining drive-in movie theaters; for some families, bundling their kids into their PJs to see the latest Disney release is an annual tradition.

CAPE MAY, NEW JERSEY. Though crowded in summer, this National Historic Landmark shore town is a family-friendly place with its Atlantic beaches and its many restaurants, Victorian bed and breakfasts (many with guest suites), and three-mile promenade. Its county park has a zoo, playground, and picnic area.

JACKSON HOLE, WYOMING. You can take in the wildlife of Yellowstone and Grand Teton national parks along with wagon train rides, hiking, biking, and, in winter, horse-drawn sleigh rides and skiing at giant Jackson Hole Mountain Resort.

MONTREAL, ONTARIO. This friendly, cosmopolitan city with European flair has lots to do and plenty of family-friendly hotels that offer weekend packages. The Parc du Mont-Royal Garden has an Insectarium with a butterfly room and more than 250,000 species of bugs. Granby Zoo has more than 1,000 animals, a children's zoo, and a new water park with family water games.

MYRTLE BEACH, SOUTH CAROLINA. Sandy white beaches line the boardwalk here. There are many large hotels, the Family Kingdom Amusement Park, an alligator farm, dozens of attractions, nature, museums, shopping, and family-friendly restaurants— just don't schedule your visit during Harley Week.

ORLANDO, FLORIDA. Although Walt Disney World may be overwhelming for toddlers, it ranks high among some families with preschoolers, who are mesmerized by seeing their favorite characters from animated Disney films come alive. The Kennedy Space Center in Cape Canaveral, an hour's drive east of Orlando, is another wonderful destination for preschoolers and parents alike.

SAN DIEGO, CALIFORNIA. Like many cities, San Diego is chockablock with things to see and do, but here, many are designed for families—so if you've got older siblings as well as little ones, it's a good bet. Everyone loves SeaWorld, the San Diego Zoo and its Wild Animal Park, Scripps Aquarium, and Balboa Park, with a number of museums, not to mention the miles and miles of Pacific Coast beaches. And the climate is nearly perfect.

SAN FRANCISCO, CALIFORNIA. Toddlers and preschoolers enjoy the crooked staircases, the winding streets, the cable cars, and the brightly painted Victorian houses, among other sights. The Exploratorium, recommended for kids aged two and up, has set the standard among interactive science museums for decades; the creativity on view entertains adults as well as their offspring. It's also fun to stop by Fisherman's Wharf and to see the sea lions near the Cliff House.

ST. LOUIS, MISSOURI. The zoo in this easy-going Midwestern town is one of the best around and there are plenty of parks and a children's museum. The immense Clydesdale horses are on display at the Anheuser-Busch estates.

BEACH VACATIONS

A beach vacation with kids can be restful and low-key. Whether you headquarter in a big resort, a townhouse development, or a seaside cottage, you don't have to change hotels from day to day, and on any given day, once you've staked your umbrella in the sand, you don't have to budge. Constant vigilance is essential at the water's edge, of course. The place you stay makes a big difference; make your arrangements eight months or more in advance to get your choice of accommodations on your choice of dates if you are traveling to southern Florida in winter or to California or the Mid-Atlantic, New England, North Florida, and Texas coasts in summer, particularly in August.

With babies

Place your baby in the shade of a sun umbrella, wearing a sun hat, and slathered with sunscreen, with her favorite toys arrayed in a portable crib set up on the sand, and you can have a great time together—tickling her tummy, playing games, looking at the seagulls and the waves, and scooping sand and water into a pail. Babies also like to sit and splash at the water's edge, if the waves are gentle. Beaches at lakes, ponds, and bays work better than Atlantic and Pacific ocean beaches, with their bigger surf. You can have a long walk down the beach together as well, with her in a frontpack or a backpack. You may even be able to snooze in the sun or read as she naps, just as you might have done before she arrived in your life.

With toddlers

The salt air and soothing sound of the ocean lulls small children into long naps—when they're not wearing themselves out running back and forth to the water's edge and making as much noise as they want. With all that room to run and play, the funny, comforting feel of warm sand under their feet, shells they can collect and take home, and seagulls to feed, the beach can be exhilarating for toddlers. They will enjoy "helping" you build castles in the sand, although the labor may be mostly yours. In calm water, you can give them inner tubes and floaties and stand by them as they experience the wonder of buoyancy—remembering, of course, that these devices are not life preservers and that you can't take your eyes off your little nonswimmer for a second. Some toddlers love jumping off the edge of a dock into your waiting arms.

With preschoolers

Preschoolers can spend hours collecting flotsam and jetsam from along the shore—building a collection of coquina shells, white rocks, flat rocks, sea glass, whatever strikes their fancy. They have real ideas about how you should build your sand castle and what features it should have, and they can be important partners in its construction. At lake and pond beaches, they may devise elaborate systems of ditches to channel water from one place to the next and cooperate with each other in the building. If there's a dock, they'll spend hours jumping off the edge and climbing back up; you'll be glad if they have good swimming skills. Some resort areas offer Red Cross swimming courses, and this is a good time to sign your children up, if they haven't started learning already. At surfy beaches, youngsters may do some splashing in the waves. In case of rainy or cool weather, you may want to look for a beach area where there's something to do away from the beach—bowling, museums, puppet shows, movie theaters, bingo, or the like. The biggest challenge is tearing yourself away when it's time to go back home.

CITY VACATIONS

Crammed with wonderful things to see and do that can be appreciated in many ways, cities are a really good option for families with young children. You can soak up some culture and people-watch while you're pushing your baby or toddler in a stroller, and, with older young ones, alternate between active pleasures like swimming pools and playgrounds and cultural activities like museums. Plus, cities are fun in almost any weather.

With babies

While your baby is small enough to be in a carrier, you can plan more or less the same itinerary you would have when it was just the two of you—provided you plan to hit museums during nap times. At other times, you can put her in a stroller and take in outdoor sights and green spaces. Inexpensive ethnic eateries and the kind of trendy restaurants that are big and noisy are easy to find, so you can even eat out.

With toddlers

Zoos, parks with pigeons, state-of-the-art playgrounds, indoor play areas in malls, and children's museums score high marks with toddlers. In fact, the Central Park and Riverside Park playgrounds in New York City are two of the city's standout attractions; they're innovative and as much fun for parents as they are for their offspring. Because some toddlers may find urban bustle overwhelming, you may want to pick a small, quiet hotel in a more residential neighborhood.

With preschoolers

At this age children not only enjoy city zoos and pigeons but are also ready for short visits to art, natural history, and science museums. If your child has been learning about a subject like dinosaurs in nursery school or is currently fixated on some movie or other, a museum with collections on that topic are instantly relevant. Some children have the temperament, attention span, and interest to stay longer than others.

BUSINESS TRIPS

Yes, you can take your child on a business trip—more and more traveling parents are doing it. Those that allow you free time certainly lend themselves to taking your offspring more readily than ones with all-day meetings that keep you apart until bedtime. But both may be preferable to prolonged separation.

With babies, you may want to take a trusted caregiver and choose accommodations that work for her as well as for you—hotels near a park, playground, or other interesting things to do, with appropriate restaurant facilities. Find out if there are highchairs and booster seats, whether the atmosphere is child-friendly, and whether the caregiver likes the type of food served. That matters if no other options are nearby.

Your toddler or preschooler may be quite excited to travel with you, even more so if you can piggy-back a short family vacation onto the trip. Some large hotels that cater to business travelers have child-care and recreational programs—which may mean other children for yours to play with. Program or not, you'll want to take your caregiver as a companion for your child when you're working.

With preschoolers, especially, you and your caregiver may do better if other diversions are on the property or nearby—a swimming pool (an indoor pool if you're traveling in cold weather), buffet meals, a movie theater, a mall with a diverse food court, museums, and so on. Your caregiver needs access to transportation for any diversions beyond walking distance.

SKI VACATIONS

The tiniest people are all over the slopes nowadays—sometimes tethered to their parents but not always. Skiing might even be the sort of fun activity you decide to take up after you've had children. Start everybody out when the kids are young, and you can all grow together in your skills; by the time your kids are 10, they may be coaching you down the slopes instead of the other way around.

One of the other great things about skiing as a family activity is that in ski resort towns, most hotels are set up for families, and restaurants are accustomed to welcoming families; you can go almost anywhere. Larger hotels have pools and other amenities that can be fun for all.

With babies

If skiing is something you like to do or think you would like to do, babyhood is not too early to introduce your offspring to snow country. Once your child is past infancy, she may enjoy sitting briefly in the snow and feeling the white stuff around her. She'll probably enjoy the spectacle of snowflakes drifting down through the air. However, you won't want to take her on the slopes with you, so if you want to ski, you will need child care. Find out what's available at the ski area and at your hotel, and consider whether you want to go with one of these options; when evaluating them, make sure there's a separate area for infants and for toddlers and preschoolers. If you plan to travel during a school holiday period, make sure that a slot is available and reserve ahead. Alternatively, you might take your own sitter, take turns skiing with your spouse, or go with another family and share baby duty. In addition, although your baby will not be spending much time outside, you may want to consult your pediatrician about your ski-trip plans since extremely cold weather isn't the best for babies.

With toddlers

For the very young, many ski resorts have day care programs with and without ski lessons as a component. Some programs start two-year-olds on skis, while others keep outdoor activities restricted to an outdoor playground until they're three and offer simple day care to younger kids, with hourly, half-day and full-day rates. Some experienced-skier parents of older toddlers give their kids a jump-start on the sport by putting them in a special harness, which is attached to a long leash, so that they can slide ahead of their parents, who hold the other end of the leash and snowplow downhill to keep the pace slow. If your skiing skills are not up to that, your ski experience with your toddler is apt to focus on the pleasures of the snow—making snowballs and snow angels, catching flakes as they fall, and building snowmen. As for the skiing, it's low-key. A ski lesson at this age usually involves fitting the kids with ski boots, bundling them into snow gear, and trundling them out to a special learning area that's just gently tilted, where they're taught to stand upright on skis, to do a snowplow to slow down and stop, and to pick themselves up when they fall. Usually kids are asked to slide towards oversized cut-out cartoon characters. Typically, short stints outside alternate with sojourns among the blocks, crayons, and toys inside. There are breaks for juice, milk and cookies, and lunch. Some toddlers have a good time with the skiing component; others don't like the structure and prefer the indoor play. It's essential to call the resort to discuss the program with a staff member. Some require that every participant be potty-trained; others can handle the diaper changes. You may want to ask about the indoor activities, naptimes, and the ratio of children to caregivers; be sure to find out whether you need reservations and if so, whether they're available on the dates you plan to visit. Once you know the scene, figure out whether you'd prefer to bring your own baby-sitter instead, or trade child care with your spouse or another family with a toddler.

With preschoolers

By now, your child has the motor skills and balance to really enjoy the slopes as well as the snow, but snow play looms large and in ski towns there are usually sleigh rides, sledding, snow-tubing, ice skating, animal-watching snowshoe treks for kids, and lots of other cold-weather activities that are fun for the whole family. As for the skiing itself, if you are just learning, you won't be equipped to teach your beginner offspring, so it's off to ski school they go. Especially if you're staying a week, do some probing into the setup of the program. In the best of them, your child is put with an instructor and a group of other children with similar abilities and stays with that group for the duration; such consistency promotes learning—after all, that's what you're paying for. Even in programs that aren't set up this way, remember that your kids will get the most attention midweek and outside of school vacation periods, and schedule yourself accordingly. While you're asking about the program, also find out how many hours your youngster will spend on skis, get the ratio of students to instructors and make sure you're comfortable with it, and confirm that the latter are certified by the Professional Ski Instructors Association.

CRUISES

A vacation on a cruise ship can be supremely relaxing. On the one hand, there are all kinds of facilities for you and your spouse, everything from spas and casinos to Bingo, lectures, and dancing; for your offspring, most cruise lines provide supervised activities for children of different ages as well as nurseries and baby-sitting. So it's easy to carve out time just for the two of you. Providing you reserve in advance, highchairs, booster seats, and cribs are all available. And there are swimming pools and many other facilities that you can all enjoy together. You also get to see a number of different and colorful destinations—without packing and unpacking from one to the next. No wonder a third of all cruisers are traveling *en famille*.

Ask your travel agent to give you some ideas about likely ships, and solicit recommendations from friends who have cruised with children the age of yours. Then study the brochures for the ships you're considering. Scope out its amenities and try to figure out whether the ship has a general atmosphere that will suit you.

Pricing is one of the big pluses of cruising as a vacation. The size and location of your stateroom is a prime determinant, but cruises are like giant all-inclusive resorts—just add water. You can find something to suit, no matter what your budget, and accommodations, meals, daytime activities, evening parties, and entertainment are all included. It's often the extras, not the basics, that inflate travel budgets—cruises keep them under control or eliminate them almost entirely. Sometimes even shore excursions, massages, and drinks are included as well. Moreover, most lines offer discounts for kids between two and 18, with even lower rates for children under two.

With babies

Can you bring a baby on your cruise? Depends on your child's age, the cruise line, and the destination. Sometimes the minimum age is four months, sometimes six, sometimes 12, and sometimes 18 months. Some ships provide disposable diapers (although there may be a limit on the number of diapers they'll give you), name-brand formula and baby food free at the purser's desk; elsewhere you have to bring your own or buy supplies on board—at premium prices. Get the scoop in advance and plan accordingly.

With toddlers and preschoolers

A great kids' program can be memorable for your youngsters and allow you some time to let your hair down. However, it's worth noting that although most ships have something, some ships are better than others for families with young children: sometimes two-year-olds are welcomed in the kids' programs while on other ships, no children younger than three can participate. The number of youth counselors and/or caregivers per child varies (a one to three ratio is ideal), as do the children's center operating hours. Find out if individual baby-sitting is available and at what price—most ships charge $8 per hour for the first child, with surcharges for additional children and a minimum of four hours; see if this can be booked at the last minute or must be reserved well in advance. Ask carefully about the accommodations you will find aboard; the bunk beds in some family rooms may or may not suit your kids and if you need a crib, make sure that you can get one—and that the cabin you might choose will be spacious enough to hold it. At mealtimes, some ships seat families with other families. Some have kids' tables, and they may be optional or standard; most have kids' menus, but not all do. The ship's itinerary and shore excursions are also something to consider when planning a family cruise. If shore excursions involve arduous hikes through hilly terrain, this cruise may not be for you. Some ships offer special excursions designed for different age groups, as well as special discounts for kids who go on regular excursions.

IF YOU'RE A SINGLE PARENT

You have many options. With babies and toddlers, you'll want to explore ideas that give you a chance to both be with your child and have some time for yourself as well. Consider a destination near a family member or close friend who will be happy to look after your child while you go to a day spa, visit a museum, or take in a movie by yourself. If you can afford it, take a caregiver your baby knows. Or travel with another single parent and child, so the adults can help each other. With toddlers, staying at an all-inclusive resort or large hotel with child care also gives you some flexibility. When your child is preschool age, you can easily plan a vacation that combines both your interests. Beach and mountain resorts and new cities are all possibilities. Be sure that the dining options are child-friendly without limiting you to coffee shops or fast food. If you think you might want to slip out for a grown-up movie, look into the availability of baby-sitting.

CAMPING AND HIKING

Family nature vacations can be blissful, a perfect way to bond. Children love to be out in nature, and they're so close to the ground and so observant that they notice all kinds of leaves, insects, rocks, and bugs that you probably don't think much about in your workaday life. It's fun to discover this natural world all over again, and some families make a tradition of camping vacations right from the start.

With babies

With a frontpack or backpack, you can take your baby on a hike almost as easily as you can pack a picnic lunch and enjoy your stroll together whether she's asleep or awake, enjoying the changing view of the woods from her perch in your carrier. Camping in drive-in campgrounds is an easy option; throw your gear into your trunk and set up a tent at one of the sites and enjoy the sights and sounds of living closer to nature (while you have your diapers and baby supplies stowed conveniently in your car, easily accessible). An overnight during mild weather, close to home, makes a good introduction.

With toddlers

In addition to bringing you amazing bits of nature along with the occasional bit of human debris, toddlers will make friends with the whole campground if you let them. As you trail around after them, you will appreciate their effect as an instant ice-breaker. If you have any doubts about whether your toddler will take to sleeping under canvas, pitch a tent in your own backyard as a dry run. If toilet training is underway or a recent accomplishment, look for a more developed campground, with flush toilets that are similar to those you have at home, and try to snag a site that's not too far from the bathrooms. If parking is not right at your site, look for a space that's also near the parking lot so that you're not lugging stuff miles into the campground. Even if your toddler's backpack contains nothing but her blankie or stuffed toy, have her carry it so that she feels she's part of the camping experience. And don't forget to bring along a portable potty just in case.

Hikes can be fun, but during their toddler years, children don't always have the stamina you might expect when you ask them to walk along a trail—and they're heavy to carry. Do take a backpack carrier just in case, and keep your plans modest—two to three miles round trip is more than enough.

With preschoolers

Whether hiking or backpacking, preschoolers may expect to carry their own backpack, complete with snacks, drinks, compass, and canteen. Your child may also enjoy having her own pair of binoculars and a magnifying glass. It's best to hike on mostly level, well-marked trails and to plan for modest walks that won't exhaust her. You may want to plan a brief trip first before you try a week in the woods.

THEME PARK VACATIONS

Parents usually fall into two camps when it comes to bringing their under-fives to amusement parks: They either can't wait to plan their first family vacations or they'd rather go anyplace else in the world. Before you plan a theme park trip, either large or small, consider your child's personality carefully and assess the best age for her to have the most enjoyable experience. At $50 and up per ticket per day, you don't want to miss a thing.

With babies

If you really, really want to visit a theme park, don't let having a baby stop you—the major parks, at least, have Baby Swap areas, so that you take turns riding and doing baby care after you've waited in line to ride together. However, this does mean that although it's feasible to take thrill rides as a young parent, you won't be sharing the experience with your spouse but will be riding, instead, with strangers—and that does get a little old. And the loud noises, crowds, and constant din won't give much pleasure to a baby, although she will certainly enjoy the music and lights of the parades, and spending time with you around the baby pool at your hotel. In general, summers are hot and parks are jam-packed; in December and during school holiday periods, crowds remain thick although weather is cooler.

With toddlers

Depending on your child's personality and attention span, the toddler years can be a good time to try out a park that is small in scale like Sesame Place outside Philadelphia. The small-fry areas of water parks are sure to please with their splashing fountains and gentle slides. Major theme parks, with their crowds and long lines, remain too overwhelming unless you go off season. Meals with costumed characters are a big draw around Orlando, and they generally delight children from toddlers on up. But because the characters' exaggerated size can make them a bit scary, you may be better off to schedule this event not at the beginning of your stay but at the end, after your youngsters have had more than one chance to eyeball the characters from a distance and get accustomed to their looks. Whichever size park you choose, keep in mind that your child will likely be attracted to different things than you are, and may even want to repeat a favorite ride, even if it entails repeated long waits in line. You're more likely to have a successful family experience if you try to see the park through your child's eyes and appreciate her pleasure, setting aside your own wishes.

With preschoolers

Four- and five-year-olds are still young enough to be mesmerized by the fantasy laid out before them in the rides and attractions. At best, they will be delighted with the detail and the characters and storybook worlds brought to life before their eyes. Intense physical sensations can make them truly sick to their stomach, and intense special effects—darkness, sudden loud noises, and anything that an adult would consider humorously spooky—can leave the more timid truly frightened. Heat and lines can provoke whines. You may want to take in thrill rides that they're not large enough or physically and mentally sturdy enough to tackle, and you'll have to put your own druthers on hold—and that may be frustrating at a place like Walt Disney World, if you suspect that you may not be able to return for a while. Still, your children's memories of the trip will be vivid and long-lived. And as you see how much they took away from this trip, the frustration may fade. To have the most successful trip, don't try to see and do too much and plan on going back another year.

ON A BUDGET?

It really is possible to travel with little ones without breaking the bank. As long as your destination isn't an expensive city or a pricey resort in high season, chances are good that you can travel almost anywhere for less than you might expect.

Visiting Friends and Relatives

Chances are that grandparents, aunts and uncles, and cousins will be delighted to play with your baby while you and your spouse catch up on your sleep, go to a movie, or have a meal out. You can count on a kitchen, laundry facilities, and the comforts of home, even if it's not yours, as a base for sightseeing. If you visit regularly, you may want to buy a new highchair, a new baby dish, portable crib, and potty chair to create a home-away-from home. Then all you'll need to take on the airplane is your diaper bag and car seat.

Camping

Once you have acquired equipment, camping is inexpensive and affordable. Campground fees are usually modest, and beyond food and some laundry, you'll have little to spend money on. Borrow equipment from co-workers, friends, and relatives until you're sure you want to make this kind of trip a permanent part of your family's travel life.

RV Travel

Renting a recreational vehicle may seem expensive at first. But because your RV serves as both lodging and transportation, it can be economical. Refrigerator and

When our daughters were three and one, we went to Los Angeles with our best friends from college who had a seven-year-old and four-year-old. We stayed as houseguests with another set of college friends, where we had use of their pool, kitchen, laundry, etc. We were especially lucky to have a kitchen available to prepare breakfast and lunch for the children, as well as have snacks for them whenever they needed. It worked out perfectly for the week that we were there. When we visited places like the La Brea tar pits, Disneyland, and Knott's Berry Farm, different adults took turns holding tired children, so no one was worn out.

—*Joy S., Salt Lake City, Utah*

stove enable you to cook your own meals and save money on food. With crawling babies and curious toddlers, you may feel safer than in a tent. And children like RVs for their novelty, in contrast to a boring old car. When you rent, keep in mind the following:

- What does your own insurance coverage include? What is the minimum additional liability coverage you might need?
- Does your rental fee include unlimited mileage? If mileage is not unlimited, what are the charges?
- Is 24-hour service provided if you break down?

House Swapping and House Rentals

One of the best ways to control expenses is to explore your destination from the base of a home exchange or a rental house—the latter is somewhat more expensive but still costs less than lodging in a hotel or motel. Sharing with another family can cut your costs even further.

KID-SAVVY TRAVEL AGENTS

Even if you've always made all the reservations yourself, consider using a travel agent for planning your family vacations. Travel agents know which destinations are child-friendly and where children are welcomed like the plague. A good travel agent can get you the best airfare and research the most attractive deals— you can do this yourself, of course, but it takes time, and that may be in short supply. Plus, travel agents know things that may be hard to find out yourself, like the capacity of different models of rental cars and whether they're large enough to accommodate your stroller, car seat, and all your other paraphernalia.

A good travel agent can give you advice on which hotel chains have the best facilities for small children, whether you're looking for a hostelry with an indoor swimming pool, a playground, a casual coffee shop, or room service pizza. Savvy agents know how the various hotel child-care programs compare, too.

If your vacation time is flexible, travel agents advise you on the best, and least costly, time to visit certain destinations. They can steer you to Europe with your preschooler in early spring or fall instead of during the hectic summer, and encourage you to go to theme parks off-season, when older children are in school. No busy parent can think of everything, and travel agents may consider details that you forget, such as making sure you'll find the crib, room refrigerator, and coin-op laundry you need when you get there.

TIMING IS ALL

Choose your travel dates carefully. If your offspring are all under five, you're in the enviable position of being able to travel whenever it suits you, unlike families with kids in school who pretty much have to vacation when every other family with school-age kids is vacationing. Planes, roads,

restaurants, hotels, and attractions experience peak crowds then, so if you can travel at any other time, it's a wise move.

Having a travel agent make the arrangements gives you some valuable protections as well. Should you be bumped from a flight or given a less-than-satisfactory hotel room, your travel agent's complaint may register more strongly with the airline or hotel, and may result in a more prompt response and more satisfactory resolution to your problem.

Note that because airlines have reduced their commissions, most agents today charge fees for airline tickets—an average of $13 per ticket in 2000, according to the American Society of Travel Agents (ASTA). Fees for other services range from nothing to $30, according to the ASTA. In general, larger agencies charge higher fees.

To find the right agent for you, ask trusted relatives and friends with children for recommendations. If you don't feel confident with your agent, don't hesitate to start over with a new one. Remember, part of the responsibility of planning a satisfying trip with a travel agent falls on you as well. The more homework you do about your destination and the more specifically you identify your desires, the better help you will get.

QUALITIES OF A GOOD TRAVEL AGENT

- ☐ Experience with the type of trip you're planning.

- ☐ A personal style that you're comfortable with.

- ☐ A cheerful, patient, and clear communication style.

- ☐ Good listening ability.

- ☐ Interest in your individual priorities.

- ☐ Full of good ideas for saving money and traveling more efficiently.

- ☐ Competitive rates.

- ☐ Membership in ASTA.

- ☐ Accreditation as a Certified Travel Consultant (CTC), earned via two years of study and five years of experience, a plus.

Give Us Shelter

MANY TODDLERS LOVE GOING to hotels and are captivated by riding the elevator or escalator up and down and watching television in a room that's not at their house. A swimming pool never fails to delight.

More to the point, though, great family trips begin with kids who are comfortable emotionally and physically. A child who feels secure sleeps well, and a child who is well-rested acclimates more readily to new surroundings and new activities than a child who is not. Moreover, if your baby isn't sleeping, you can bet that you won't either. So on the sleep front alone, finding family-friendly accommodations and making them as home-like as possible is vital.

Choice of accommodations affects your trip in other ways. If you're traveling with toddlers and preschoolers, staying at a place where your offspring can mingle with his peers—as you exchange parenting sagas with fellow moms and dads from other cities—can enrich your experience immeasurably. If you want to spend time alone, just the two of you, a child-care program or ready access to baby-sitting that you trust can make it much easier to carve out those few private moments.

Price, setting, amenities and activities, and how much space you need continue to figure in the choice. Trying to make the best choice for your whole family may steer you toward options that you would never have considered as a twosome but that will ultimately reveal new and rewarding dimensions of your destination.

FINDING THE BEST
HOTEL FOR YOUR FAMILY

When you start to sort out all the options, there are three main areas to consider—the hotel's location, its facilities and amenities, and the rooms themselves.

Location, Location, Location

When you're traveling with small children, convenience is paramount. Staying in the heart of the city enables you to quickly duck outside for a stroll if your baby starts howling at dawn. It also reduces the number of items you'll have to carry around in your daypack because, after a morning museum visit or walking tour, you can pop back in to your hotel for a quick nap or snack. And it makes it easier to get to most places you want to go at a time of your life when just getting out the door can be a challenge.

Of course the more convenient the hostelry the more expensive it will usually be. Hotels that are close to the middle of town in many urban areas just cost more. At the beach, an oceanfront hotel is usually more expensive. In theme park land, the closest to the main park entrance command the highest prices. Normally you get a little bit more for your money in addition to the location; at theme parks, properties that are the most convenient also have play and picnic areas, lavish kiddie pools, and menu items inspired by favorite cartoon characters.

Occasionally, though, you may want to headquarter away from the city center. Hotels just off the highway usually have large parking lots, and if you want to have ready access to strollers, portable highchairs, and other items you might not need to unpack for the room, you might prefer to stay at one of these hostelries with an accessible parking lot.

Amenities

Amenities always count when picking a hotel, but when kids are involved, the way you prioritize those amenities may change. It's not so much about what the place looks like or whether they put a chocolate on your pillow at night so much as it is about whether the hotel can enhance your experiences as a family. An indoor or outdoor pool can provide hours of fun for all of you together, becoming a focal point for your visit. The same goes for a playground at the hotel or nearby—and remember, it doesn't take much to enchant a baby or toddler. You may also want to ask if the hotel has a children's program, because this means that your kids are likely to find playmates.

It's practical to look for laundry facilities, especially if you're staying for a while. Also ask about cribs or roll-away beds and inquire as to whether restaurants at the hotel have booster seats or highchairs.

Find out if there's baby-sitting service or if the hotel can help you find a sitter if you think you might want one. If you want to put your child to sleep and then be able to eat a nice meal, room service from a really good on-site restaurant may be a necessity rather than a luxury. And after you've put the baby down, you may enjoy catching a movie on cable TV or a pay-per-view movie.

Rooms

When selecting rooms for small children, always ask for the largest available so you can unpack, spread out, and still be comfortable. Think about bed configuration. Does it make more sense to reserve a king-size bed and put your child in the middle or would two doubles suffice?

You may also want to consider the bathroom setup and kitchen facilities. For example, if your child has never taken a shower before, you will probably want a room with a bathtub. A kitchenette or at least refrigerator and microwave will come in handy when you need to fix your child a snack or warm up some formula.

Ask if rooms are adequately ventilated and have operable windows. Without fresh air, rooms can be dry and babies' nasal passages can become irritated.

Look for room locations that make sense for kids. Quarters at the end of a hallway are good because there's less chance you'll disturb other guests if the baby cries—or be disturbed by other guests as they make their way to and from their rooms. If the streets are noisy or brightly lit at night, you may want to request a room that faces an interior courtyard so your baby or toddler won't be suddenly wakened by outside noise. And if you want to increase the chances that your toddler will sleep in, try for a room facing west or north, one that won't catch the first rays of dawn. For safety's sake, avoid balconies. If you have a lot of gear to haul in and out of the room, go for a hostelry that has at-door parking, or at least a room that's close to the door. That way, you'll have a shorter distance to carry your paraphernalia.

HOMES AWAY FROM HOME

Sorting out the options takes a little doing. Motel? Hotel? Resort? Rental apartment? Home exchange? Your options are many and more varied than you might expect.

All-Suite Hotels

In an increasing number of newer hotels every room is a suite, and you will usually find a good blend of amenities, value, and kid-friendliness. Suites generally include a separate sleeping area or bedroom (and sometimes two), a living room with a dining area, and a fully equipped kitchen. Many include a full breakfast in the morning, and a minibar stocked with (pricey) beverages and snacks. Other amenities include playgrounds or play equipment, children's camps, activities such as crafts classes, a shopping service to stock the refrigerator, multiple TVs, complimentary cocktails, and sports and exercise facilities. With 24-hour notice, some chains provide baby-sitting referrals. The price for all this may not exceed that of a standard hotel room, and package deals can reduce the rate even more.

Motels and Motor Hotels

Officially a motel is one of those modern one- to three-story hostelries where the room doors open onto outside corridors. If you're staying on the ground floor, you can access the trunk of your car just steps from your door. Although a charming B&B may be the accommodation of your dreams, you can't argue with the convenience of a simple motel. With a toddler in tow, you might want to make the next step up on the lodging ladder and go for a motor hotel, which has inside hallways that lead to—as your toddler will see it—exotic and entertaining spaces like the lobby, the dining room, the pool, and so on. Motor hotels are far less confining.

Budget Options

Budget hostelries, both motels and motor hotels, have affordable rates but fewer amenities. You can expect air conditioning, TV, and a pool in most cases, but anything else is a bonus. Even wall-to-wall carpets aren't assured, which may be an issue with crawling babies or in cold seasons.

To save money, look for family rates, special weekend rates, AAA rates, and other deals at fancier hostelries. Package deals may include free breakfast, pizza dinners, pay-per-view movies, or tickets for a local movie theater. Some hotels allow children even as old as 18 to stay in their parents' room for free. Some allow children under 12 to eat at the hotel restaurant for free. If you plan to stay in one place for awhile, some hotels and motels sell weekly rates. Inquire about all these possibilities.

Bed and Breakfasts

Bed and breakfasts are private homes or small, family-operated inns that have rooms available for rent. Often, they are architecturally attractive, impeccably maintained, and in scenic areas or other places that greatly appeal to tourists. B&Bs usually cost more than motels but are more homey. Many discourage or even ban children under the ages of 10. But not all.

To find a B&B that works for your family, start by asking the proprietor if kids are OK. Look for a welcoming attitude, not mere tolerance. Cribs or cots available for the bedrooms, play areas and equipment outside, and a highchair or booster seat available in the dining room are signs of kid-friendliness. You'll also want to know whether separate rooms for kids and adults are available, whether bathrooms are private or shared with other guests, whether the price includes breakfast, and whether the breakfast is full or continental. Find out about the knickknack quotient—you'll be very unhappy in a B&B full of breakables if you're visiting with a toddler. Also find out about the breakfast; make sure that accommodations can be made for your youngster if she's a fussy eater.

You can find B&Bs written up in travel guidebooks; friends are another good source of leads, particularly friends who have traveled to their recommendations with their own kids.

Home Rentals and Exchanges

Home exchanges refer to an arrangement whereby you swap primary residences or vacation homes with another family that wants to travel at the same time you do. Both rentals and home exchanges have a big advantage, at least from your child's point of view. When you rent or exchange homes, that usually means you're staying for awhile in one place rather than hopping from hotel to hotel. This relaxed form of travel may help your kids feel more secure.

Rentals and exchanges have other practical advantages. You'll likely have more room and privacy than you would at a hotel and the amenities may even exceed those of your own home. Having a full kitchen makes it possible to prepare all or most of your meals, which not only saves you money but gives you more control over your diet. You'll also have laundry facilities. Depending on your vacation needs, consider convenience versus cost when renting or exchanging a home.

It takes more effort to arrange rentals and exchanges than hotel rooms. You can't just call up and make a reservation. You'll find exchanges, and sometimes rentals, through directories published by exchange clubs or Web sites such as International Home Exchange Network. You can find rentals through publications and Web sites devoted exclusively to them such as CyberRentals. In addition, you can post notices requesting rentals to an online newsgroup, forum, or board. If you haven't used newsgroups before, start at Dejanews for help in navigating the landscape. (See Family Resources section.) Other resources include travel books, classified ads, vacation clubs, local tourist offices, travel agents, and friends, relatives, and work associates. Don't assume it's cheaper to rent from a homeowner than from commercial sources such as travel agents. Many condominium and home rental agencies pay commissions to travel agents at no additional charge to customers. Whichever source you choose, start your search six to eight months in advance (or more) for an exchange or rental during high season, at least two months ahead off-season.

Exchanges require some serious matchmaking, starting with narrowing down places available for your dates. Continue the process by identifying properties that interest you most. Entries in exchange directories or Web sites contain the basic information you need on the location, the family that lives there, and available options (such as access to a car or boat). Send the owner a letter or e-mail that describes your own home, family, and community in detail. Include descriptions of nearby amenities and activities (playgrounds, parks, beaches, theme parks, recreation, etc.) and your local climate. Also list your preferred dates for exchanging and ask questions not answered by the owner's entry. For instance, is the neighborhood safe for your child to play outside? If the property is a condominium, ask about the policy on children—there's sure to be one. Also inquire about activities, services, and facilities on-site and whether there is on-site management or a manager who visits. (If the latter, how frequently?) If you send a letter, include a self-addressed, stamped envelope to make it easy for the owner to reply.

Once you've found a possible match, finding out a few more details will help in making your decision. For example, a family who has kids the same age as yours will most likely have compatible playthings, crib, and so on. You may also want to ask about housekeeping standards, care of equipment, and so on.

Tie down your agreement with a letter that includes dates of the exchange, number of people in both families, everything (facilities, services, vehicles, etc.) that you understand is included by the other homeowner, and everything you're including on your end. Regarding your own property, your letter should also cover fees if any (say, for pool-cleaning or housekeeping service) and insurance coverage on house and vehicles.

Before you take off, write down for your guest family all the pertinent information regarding care and use of your home and other useful items about your community. You should cover pet care, cleaning instructions, how to handle telephone and utility bills, children's policies and other covenants (if exchanging a condo or house in a planned community), use and care of household equipment (washer, dryer, dishwasher, sound system, pool, answering machine, and so on), suggested activities and amenities nearby, and house and vehicle insurance contact information. Provide a list of phone numbers for emergencies, automobile repair, local physicians, friends and neighbors who know the house and community, and baby-sitters. (You may want to store this information in a computer for future exchanges.) Staple all the information together so it forms a booklet and make several more copies. You should also request similar information from the family whose home you will be occupying.

Arranging a rental is much the same in many respects. Contact the rental agency or the owner and find out about availability on your preferred dates. Then ask about the property's amenities and setting. Is there a dishwasher? A grill? A washer/dryer? A VCR? How many bathrooms? How many bedrooms and what kind of beds are there? Does the house come with a crib and a highchair, if you need them, or must you bring your own? What are the views? How close is the house to the road, and how busy is the road? Is there a fence? What other facilities are there outside? What's the cost? How far is the house from the beach or from any other sites you want to visit? If all systems are go, the broker or the owner will expect a deposit and ask you to sign a lease.

All-Inclusive Family Resorts

All-inclusive family resorts enable you to stay put in one place with lots of activity options, all for a single package price. The deal normally includes accommodations, meals, tips, and all activities including tennis, bicycling, horseback riding, scuba lessons, sailboating, water-skiing, and workouts with trainers. Airfare may be included or at least discounted. Budgetwise, it makes planning daily activities a snap because you know everything has been paid for up front, with no extras.

On the other hand, if you enjoy exploring new locales or sampling the local cuisine, you may find an all-inclusive limiting. Your price includes eating all your meals at the same restaurant no matter how extensive the menu and following a specific itinerary. Deviating from this itinerary usually costs extra. Also, rooms tend to be smaller than most hotel rooms because all-inclusives are designed as more activity-based, which means you'll have minimum time in your room. While many all-inclusives don't welcome children under 18, others cater to families with young children, such as Radisson Cable Beach Resort in the Bahamas, Boscobel Beach and Beaches Negril in Jamaica, Club Med Sandpiper in Florida, and Club Med Ixtapa in Mexico. Expect family-friendly all-inclusives to have child-care programs, play areas, and kids' menus at a minimum. Special activities can include swim lessons, clown school, and ice cream parties. Be sure to ask what is included before signing up.

Rates for all-inclusive range from about $150 to over $500 per day (as a rule, the more expensive resorts have

When we were vacationing in San Diego, we stayed at a family-oriented all-inclusive resort by the bay. There were lots of things for our two preschoolers to do—play on the beach, ride with us on four-wheeled family bikes, go to the children's pool, feed the ducks in the big ponds, rent small sailboats and cruise around the bay, and more. But we soon learned that our kids wanted to do what they were enjoying at the time without being pushed to move onto something else. We finally figured out that it was best to let them choose activities rather than stick to our agenda. If they were enjoying something they were doing, we let that activity run its course. And we gave them lots of free time between activities. By getting in synch with our kids' rhythms, our vacation together really hit its stride.

TRAVEL LOG

—*Barbara S., Seattle, Washington*

fancier food, more luxurious surroundings, and other extras). If the price causes sticker-shock, repeat the mantra all-inclusive and compare your savings to car rental, gas, and meals. Staying at an all-inclusive resort during off-season and maximize the number of week-days in your stay helps keep the price as low as possible. Some all-inclusive chains also sell flexible-traveler specials. You tell them which dates you'd prefer and they send you to whichever of their resorts most needs to fill vacancies, with a deep discount as your reward for being so accommodating.

WHAT TO LOOK FOR IN A FAMILY RESORT

- ☐ Price that includes all meals and tips and all activities you plan to do.
- ☐ Children's menu.
- ☐ Enough appealing activities to occupy your family during your stay.
- ☐ Well-equipped play area for children.
- ☐ Airfare included or discounted.
- ☐ Special meals or variety of on-site restaurants.
- ☐ Child-care program.
- ☐ Off-season specials.
- ☐ Flexible traveler specials.

CHILD CARE AT RESORTS AND HOTELS

When you plan a visit to a hotel or resort, look carefully at the child-care program. As when you hire a professional sitter on your own, childcare personnel should be bonded, have undergone background checks and be insured. Also ask:

▶ What is the ratio of caregiver to children? It should not exceed one to four for infants or one to ten for preschoolers.

▶ What are operating hours and costs?

▶ How much advance notice is needed to get your child a slot?

▶ What activities are planned?

▶ Do you need to provide any special clothing for your child?

▶ Can he be taken in and out of the facility throughout the day, and can you drop in to hang out with him for a while?

▶ Are siblings allowed to stay together?

▶ Are there meals and snacks? At what time? If you have dietary considerations, you'll want to know which foods are on the menu and if you can provide your own substitutions.

When you confirm arrangements, have the sitter arrive about an hour early. During this time, you can observe her interaction with your child and your child has time to get comfortable with this new person before the anxiety of your departure. Plus, you'll feel a lot better yourself if you've left your toddler happily involved.

QUESTIONS TO ASK THE BABY-SITTER

Interview the sitter before you hire her. Let her know what she can and can't do with your kids. Is it okay for her to leave the room? Use the pool? Sign for a meal in the restaurant or for room service? Find out about her previous baby-sitting experience, focusing specifically on her work with children as young as yours. Ask:

☐ Do you have references?

☐ What is your experience with children the same age as my child?

☐ Who would you call in an emergency?

☐ What would you do if my child refuses to go to bed or refuses to eat?

☐ Do you smoke?

☐ Do you know CPR?

☐ How do you plan to entertain the children?

☐ If you and I have different ideas about how a situation should be handled, which approach would you take?

SWEET DREAMS
CAN TRAVEL

If your child needs a nightlight to feel emotionally comfortable at home, pack an extra in case you lose one. If you do get stuck without, leave a nearby light on in the bathroom or closet.

Physical comfort is usually less of a challenge. You may consider having your preschooler sleep in a sleeping bag. He will probably see this as an exciting adventure; use an air mattress if you're worried about hard or cold floors.

For babies on the road, comfort is rarely a factor, but safety is. Babies often sleep just fine in the crib a hotel provides. Do make sure it meets safety standards, however: The gap between slats should not exceed 2⅜ inches; there should also not be any gap around sides of mattress. The latter problem can be handled by asking for extra blankets and stuffing them between the mattress and the sides. If the slats are too widely spaced, the crib is not safe. Ask for a room with a king-size bed and put baby in bed with you. Or if there is an extra bed in the room and your infant is not yet very mobile, push the bed against the wall and put pillows around the edge. Alternatively, you may want to travel with a portable crib. Look for one-piece, collapsible models.

On our trip to England last year with our three-year-old Jenny, I learned a trick about storytelling that has helped at home, too. Jenny was having trouble falling asleep in our hotels. I could tell she was having problems deal-

TRAVEL LOG

ing with all the new experiences from the trip but I didn't know what to do about it. I finally figured out that our daytime conversations weren't enough to sort out what happened. So I altered our bedtime story routine just enough to make the story about everything that happened that day. This end-of-day review made a huge difference. She seemed much happier when she put her head on the pillow and began sleeping through the night.

—*Jonell P., Providence, Rhode Island*

Sleep Problems

Prevent sleep problems on the road altogether by maintaining as much of your child's bedtime routine as possible while traveling. Keep to that same routine during your trip, and don't stray too far from your child's usual bedtime. The familiarity of ritual will reassure your child in his unfamiliar surroundings.

Ready, Set, Go

YOUR KIDS AREN'T THE WORLDWISE travel veterans that you are. To get them to look forward to the trip the same way you do, you have to take a few extra steps.

Get your kids psychologically up to speed for traveling with discussions, games that are rehearsals for new experiences, and even involving your children in the planning and packing if they are old enough. If your children realize that the trip is for them, too, they may even beat you out the door the day you depart.

GETTING YOUR KIDS READY FOR TRAVEL

Young children can get just as excited about travel as their parents. For instance, kids who constantly pore over their airplane books at home will probably look forward to climbing aboard a real plane and actually flying somewhere. Nevertheless, young kids are still unsure of the world and their place in it. They cling to the familiar and fear even tame unknowns. With the exception of babies, who are usually content to go anywhere that you do, youngsters will often do better on a trip if you prepare them for it beforehand.

Trip preparation should include several key steps. First, let youngsters know that the trip will include many activities that they enjoy. Second, reassure toddlers and preschoolers that their new experiences won't be scary ones. Third, expose kids to aspects of the trip that they're likely to find strange, such as foreign languages and foods, before leaving home. Fourth, don't start any new routines right before leaving home—solid foods for babies, toilet-training for toddlers, and so on.

Now comes the actual preparation. As any parent knows, small children have little sense of time—three-year-olds often begin thinking about their next birthday the day after their current one—so giving them too much advance notice about an upcoming trip can create problems. While there are plenty of ways to calm them and even get them excited about going, you don't want to start the process too early or they may cycle through the excitement and go right back to worrying. On the other hand, you can't just pack their suitcase and pop them into a car or plane. The following recommendations will help you prepare your child for travel.

For Toddlers

▶ Give advance notice. Changes in routine may upset very young children. They know something is afoot when suitcases emerge from closets and a new sense of urgency is in the household. Don't break the news about the trip after your trip preparations are already obvious to your child. That said, you shouldn't need more than a few weeks of advance notice and less may do, especially with pre-verbal toddlers who tend to live very much in the present.

▶ Explain the trip. At this age especially, children often feel much better about whatever they're doing if they understand what will be happening. Explain the steps of the trip, including what they need to know about packing; what will happen when the taxi or van comes to take the family to the airport; what it's like to check in, wait at a gate, and board the plane at an airport; and what you're all going to see together when you reach your destination.

▶ Rehearse the unfamiliar. Use let's-pretend games to role-play unfamiliar experiences. For instance, take a make-believe trip in your living room, transforming the couch into a car or plane, so your child can have a feel for what will be happening. Or let your toddler or preschooler pack a suitcase for a pretend journey, cut up pieces of colored paper for pretend

TRAVEL LOG

To get James, our two-year-old, ready for his first airplane flight, my husband, Tim, took him out to the car and pretended it was a plane. He buckled James into his car seat in the back, and then Tim buckled himself into the driver's seat and played pilot. He made take-off sounds and also called out announcements like a pilot or flight attendant would. James loved it and could hardly wait for the real flight day to come.

—*Stephanie H., Tulsa, Oklahoma*

tickets, and role-play being both waitress and customer in a restaurant.

▸ Introduce distant friends and relatives. If you're going to visit friends or relatives, bring out the photo album and show your child pictures of the people you'll be seeing. Relate special memories about the people, too.

▸ Use travel-related books. Borrow or buy toddler-age books about the means of transportation and your destination, and read them to your child.

▸ Establish a comfort level. Reassure your child that no matter where she is with you, she'll still be able to do the things she likes best—reading stories, listening to tapes, playing games with you, and so on.

For Preschoolers

▸ Tell your child as soon as she's ready. It's often fine to start talking about the planning process with children of this age a few months ahead of your departure date. But that varies with the child. For a youngster with a short attention span, one who has a hard time understanding exactly how long it is until Christmas, a shorter lead time may be best. You can start the conversation earlier with a child who understands that she'll nearly finish her preschool term before leaving for Walt Disney World in the spring.

▸ Include your child in the trip-planning process. Have a session with your child one evening where you highlight maps for your trip with a magic marker. Tell her that you'll be bringing the maps along so she can help navigate.

▶ Use visual aids. Show your child magazine pictures, maps, guidebooks, and travel photos of the place you're headed to give her a sense of what you'll be seeing together.

▶ Use books and tapes. Go to the library or local bookstore together to find age-appropriate books and videos about the destination and means of transportation.

▶ Include her desires. Tell your child what kinds of activities will be available on the trip and ask her what she'd like to do and what sites she's interested in seeing, and be sure to include some of those in your plans.

▶ Take her with you to the travel agent. Take your child along when you see the travel agent to give her a chance to ask questions about the trip, or at least have some sense of what's in store.

▶ Invite imagination. Encourage your child to think about where she's going and draw pictures of things she wants to see and do. Let her choose letters or postcards to send to relatives and playmates.

▶ Involve your child's school. If you're planning a trip that will take your child out of preschool for a few days, check with your child's teacher to see if the trip can become part of the school experience, either before your child leaves or when she returns. One four-year-old who left nursery school early to travel

O ur family goes to a resort near Miami every year for the week of Christmas. Our three-year-old Bryan wasn't very excited about leaving home last year, so we pulled out a brochure of the resort and showed him pictures of the beach, the swim-

TRAVEL LOG

ming pools, the room layout including the television, and the terraced restaurant. Once he realized that he could still have plenty of fun in new surroundings, he was as ready for the change as we were.

—*Sandie W., Portsmouth, New Hampshire*

with his parents to Florence, Italy, came back with excited stories for his classmates about eating risotto.

For Both Toddlers and Preschoolers

▶ Play it again. Children love reruns of favorite experiences. If your daughter loves building sandcastles and that's on the itinerary, let her know that and she'll look forward to it. If you've been to the same place before (like an amusement park or Grandma's house), remind your child about the good times you've had there, and how much fun you'll have again.

▶ Count the days. Hang a pre-trip calendar in your kitchen or family room where your child can cross off the days until departure.

▶ Learn the lingo. If you're going to a place where the main language isn't English, borrow language tapes from the local library so your child will hear what Spanish, Italian, or Japanese sounds like. Children who are just acquiring language skills can be threatened by even short-range jaunts—say, from San Diego to Tijuana, Mexico—where the language is unfamiliar. By bringing the foreign language into your home first, you make the actual visit to the country far less strange for your child.

▶ Introduce new foods. If you're venturing somewhere where the cuisine is significantly different from what your child is used to, try to introduce some of the foods that you may be eating while you're away. Many children may be hesitant to try new flavors or foods. If you expose your child beforehand to selected items, she'll adapt more easily to different foods on the road. Keep in mind that even foods with the same names don't always taste the same in different places. For instance, farm-cooked Irish oatmeal doesn't look or taste much like the American supermarket variety, and even Mc-Donald's fare can be slightly different outside the United States.

- ▶ Introduce activities. If your family is heading somewhere to pursue an activity or sport that's new to your child, such as skiing or hiking, take her to related stores to show her some of the equipment involved and get her comfortable with the idea of joining in.

- ▶ Make a test run. If you're not sure a travel experience may work for your kids, take a trial run. Go

BEFORE-YOU-GO CHECKLIST

- ☐ Leave multiple copies of instructions for house-sitter and neighbor. Include emergency and other important phone numbers.

- ☐ Make arrangements for someone to check on your house- and pet-sitters if you don't know them well.

- ☐ Pack passports, travelers checks or enough cash, birth certificates if needed, and medical insurance information.

- ☐ Turn off your house lights and water.

- ☐ Put newspaper delivery on hold.

- ☐ Have the post office hold your mail or arrange for a neighbor to pick it up.

- ☐ Give your pets enough food and water to last until the pet-sitter arrives.

for a short walk in a nearby state park or a day-hike close to home before you commit to a trip that involves lots of trekking. Visit a local gallery before you schedule a trip to another city that involves making the rounds of major art museums.

Pets

If you have pets that will stay at home, reassure your child that the animal will be well taken care of. Preschoolers who are devoted to their pets can easily

---

I love being with my children when I travel but I also need some time just for myself as well as time alone with my husband. We work it out by going to resorts that both have good child care and good adult attractions. Some days, I'll take our preschool daughters to the pool while my husband golfs. He'll

TRAVEL LOG

take the kids at other times while I go for a pre-dinner massage. After dinner, we take the kids to child care so we can relax a little or go dancing.

—*Sharon K., Memphis, Tennessee*

---

become anxious about who will watch their hamster, fish, cat, or dog while they're away. So if you're asking a neighbor to stop by or are planning to board your pet somewhere else, be sure to include your child in that planning process. You can encourage her to make up a list of the animal's daily routines, favorite foods, and likes and dislikes to share with the caregiver. It may help ease some of your child's anxiety if you include her when you meet with the pet-sitter before leaving home.

PACKING FOR KIDS

Whether babies or five-year-olds, young children can't travel light. Not only do they run through several outfits a day, they also need diapers, cribs, strollers, toys, books, child-proofing paraphernalia, and comfort items like blankies and stuffed animals. Two questions come immediately to mind: How are you going to remember it all? And how are you going to carry so much stuff?

To answer the first question, start with the lists below and modify them to fit your own situation. Make a mental review of a typical day at home, from your child's wake-up time to her bedtime, and all the clothes and other items you use. If you keep a running list, so much the better. Start making lists several weeks before you pack in case you need to buy something—such as a portable crib or collapsible stroller.

As for how you're going to carry it all, you need to strike that delicate balance—you use everything you brought because you have brought exactly, precisely what you need, neither too little nor too much. To save space, plan to buy disposable diapers on the road, unless you're going to a foreign country where suitable diapers aren't always available.

Essentials for Babies

Carriers and strollers

Whether you bring a collapsible stroller depends a lot on where you're going and how you like to transport your child. Collapsible, umbrella-type strollers that fit in an overhead airplane compartment make the most sense. Carriages are bulkier, heavier, and less maneuverable than strollers, and most do not collapse. The more expensive strollers are sturdier and more comfortable for child and parent alike. They also open and close easier, handle better, and fit in an overhead airplane compartment. If you don't use a stroller regularly and are bound for a city where you'll be doing a lot of walking and getting in and out of taxis and buses, make sure your stroller is up to the challenge.

- Test your brakes to make sure they lock both wheels and are easy to use.
- Make sure the restraining straps—with crotch extension—are easily fastened and snug enough that your child can't slip out.
- Check that hinges and other mechanisms don't catch tiny fingers.
- Make sure that the release mechanism for closing the stroller actually works.
- Acquire sun and rain shields if you don't already have them.

You'll be happiest if your stroller handles are positioned for you to push comfortably and if you can steer and fold the stroller with one hand.

Even if you do take a stroller, a front- or backpack is a must-have item for sightseeing and general maneuvering in the world: With your baby safely ensconced, your hands are free to haul out tickets or maneuver carry-ons at airports and elsewhere.

Highchairs

You can always wing it and cope with what's available, and that's probably the best bet on short trips. If you're going to be on the road for more time, consider bringing a portable hook-on table chair. You'll have a reliable, comfortable seat that your baby is familiar with

CARRY-ON LIST FOR BABIES

- ☐ Two pacifiers
- ☐ Baby spoon
- ☐ Changing pad or square yard of clear, heavy-duty plastic
- ☐ Clothing changes
- ☐ Diaper rash cream
- ☐ Disposable diapers
- ☐ Disposable wipes or washcloths and thermos with warm water
- ☐ Extra pair of socks or booties
- ☐ Food
- ☐ Formula
- ☐ Light blanket or terry cloth towel
- ☐ Outerwear
- ☐ Two or three gallon-size resealable plastic bags
- ☐ Small toys
- ☐ Sun hat
- ☐ Sweater
- ☐ Water or juice
- ☐ Waterproof bibs

and you won't have to worry about finding highchairs in restaurants and hotels. Some models are relatively light, fold flat, and come with a tote bag.

Sleeping

Babies can sleep almost anywhere. You can either construct your own baby bed out of folded up blankets or bring a portable crib. Or take a large drawer out of one of the dressers and line it with blankets.

Food

If you plan on flying, bring baby food, since most in-flight meals are not suited to infants.

Essentials for Toddlers and Preschoolers

Comfort objects

It goes without saying that you will bring your child's blankie or favorite stuffed animal to ease her anxiety in unfamiliar environs. Or does it? Traveling parents have mixed opinions on this point because if any of your child's favorites get lost en route, you may all have problems for the rest of the trip. One school of thought is that you bite the bullet and bring Elephant or Affie anyway—and prepare to monitor the location of this precious object much as you would that of the family pet or a diamond ring. If your child's comfort object is a blanket, talk to her about tearing it in half and leaving one half at home and taking the other half on your trip.

The other bit of wisdom advises that you leave the absolute favorites at home and bring secondary favorites

PACKING LIST FOR BABIES

- ☐ Two blankets
- ☐ Two outfits per day
- ☐ Two pair of pajamas or blanket sleepers
- ☐ Two T-shirts

Also consider:

- ☐ Baby bottles
- ☐ Baby food grinder
- ☐ Baby shampoo
- ☐ Baby swing (compact when collapsed)
- ☐ Breast pump
- ☐ Baby-bottle nipples and rings
- ☐ Comb
- ☐ Formula
- ☐ Instant baby cereal
- ☐ Nail clippers
- ☐ Plug-in intercom
- ☐ Portable crib
- ☐ Portable hook-on table highchair
- ☐ Swimsuit and diaper cover

instead. Or buy special comfort items such as toys or books just for the trip, making sure your child accepts them first before you leave home. Before your first big trip together, a trial run over a weekend may be in order so that you can decide which camp you want to join.

Travel surprises

Before the trip, stockpile a number of special toys to introduce during the trip and use to occupy your child when you want time to finish your meal or take care of

ITEMS TO PACK FOR KIDS OF ANY AGE

- ☐ Camera and film
- ☐ Can opener and bottle opener
- ☐ Childproofing supplies
- ☐ Clothespins
- ☐ Extension cords
- ☐ Extra shoelaces
- ☐ Insect repellent
- ☐ Night-lights
- ☐ Sunscreen
- ☐ Travel sewing kit and scissors
- ☐ Traveling medicine chest

travel business. Because they're novel, these items may buy you more time than familiar things. Special edible treats can serve a similar purpose. Ditto for stickers, glue sticks, finger puppets, blunt scissors, pads of paper, magnetic games and puzzles, magic markers, and coloring books.

Clothing

When selecting clothes for the trip, choose items that are comfortable, suitable for the climates you'll experience, easy to launder, and quick to dry. Bring your

CARRY-ON CHECKLIST FOR TODDLERS AND PRESCHOOLERS

- ☐ Two pacifiers
- ☐ Comfort items
- ☐ Complete change of clothes
- ☐ Diapers
- ☐ Disposable wipes or washcloths and thermos of warm water
- ☐ Games, toys, and activities for the ride
- ☐ Gum or chewy foods
- ☐ Snacks
- ☐ Special food treats
- ☐ Water bottle or juice box

child's clothes in separate suitcases: pack some in your child's suitcase and some with another family member's belongings, in case one of the suitcases is lost or delayed. Carry-on clothing specific to the climate, such as a coat or extra sweater if visiting a cooler destination.

PACKING LIST FOR TODDLERS OR PRESCHOOLERS

- ☐ One dress-up outfit
- ☐ Two pair of shoes
- ☐ Three outfits per day
- ☐ Three pair of socks
- ☐ Three pair underwear
- ☐ Comb
- ☐ Diaper cover
- ☐ Diapering supplies
- ☐ Hair accessories
- ☐ Kids' toiletries
- ☐ Outerwear
- ☐ Potty seat or toilet-seat adapter
- ☐ Pull-ups
- ☐ Swimsuit
- ☐ Waterproof sheet or equivalent

Food

No matter how well you prepare your children for the new foods they'll encounter on your trip, it's a good idea to bring along some familiar mainstays from your kitchen, like cold cereal and Parmalat or another brand

FOR SKI TRIPS

☐ Dress your child in insulated bib overalls, a warm ski parka, water-resistant gloves, a neck gaiter, cotton turtleneck, and a fleece hat. He'll also need long john tops and bottoms and real ski socks—everyday cotton socks aren't warm enough. It's good to have an extra pair of gloves for him to put on later in the day—even water-resistant gloves end up wet.

☐ To prevent lift accidents, remove drawstrings from jackets and do not allow your child to wear a loose scarf that might get caught. A fleece neck gaiter is preferable. If your daughter has long hair, put it into one long braid or two pigtails.

☐ Let your preschooler wear his long johns to bed. Kids get a kick out of thinking they're going out in public dressed in their pajamas.

☐ Buy a helmet for your preschooler when he's ready to leave the learner slopes. Even if he's in control, you never know about other skiers, and it's better to be safe than sorry.

of packaged milk that doesn't need to be refrigerated. Snacks for the plane are important. Airplane food doesn't always appeal to children and you can't count on food being there when you need it. Cheerios, crackers, bananas, seedless grapes, and string cheese are good bets. Bring a bottle of water to prevent your child from getting dehydrated.

DRESSING KIDS FOR TRAVEL

Young children often fall asleep when they travel, especially on driving trips, so it's best to dress them in loose, comfortable clothing. If you expect to arrive around their bedtime, comfortable clothes have an additional advantage—you can put your sleeping child to bed in them instead of wrestling her out of her clothing. For toddlers and preschoolers, sweatpants or shorts and T-shirts make ideal basic garments, with sweaters, sweatshirts, or jackets for layering when it's cool. Keep in mind cars and airplanes can be stuffy so your child should always be able to strip down to cooler, cotton clothes if needed.

If you want to get your sleeping child into pajamas before bed, have her travel in clothes that are easy to get

COUNTDOWN TO TAKE-OFF

☐ Make sure the baby supply bag is stocked and readily accessible.

☐ Have all baby equipment lined up and ready to go.

☐ Keep children's snacks, comfort items, and surprise bag of special travel goodies in an accessible place at all times.

☐ Diaper your baby or take your toddler or pre-schooler to the bathroom before departing.

☐ Have medical records and pediatrician phone number (both for home and at your destination) accessible.

☐ Reconfirm with your accommodations (hotel, condo, or grandparents' place) that any requested special equipment (cribs, highchairs, bottle warmers, etc.) will be waiting for you.

☐ Test out any new equipment that you will be depending on during your trip.

☐ Leave your home, including your children's rooms, as neat and tidy as possible so it will be pleasant to come back to.

If flying:

☐ Whenever possible, have confirmed boarding passes.

☐ If you've ordered special kids' meals, double-check the arrangements with the airline a few days before the flight.

☐ Confirm the actual departure time before leaving home.

☐ If you asked for a smoke-free room when you booked a hotel reservation, confirm that one will be available when you check in.

on and off—pull-ons or at least clothes without a lot of buttons or other fasteners. With babies, easy on-and-off is the rule at any point in your trip because you may be changing diapers in tight quarters such as backseats of cars and airplane seats.

Merrily We Roll Along

A PLANE TRIP to the Virgin Islands. A four-hour car ride to Grandma and Grandpa's in California. A leisurely train journey through the Canadian Rockies. No matter where you're going and how you get there, successfully traveling with kids comes down to a few never-changing basics. Plan ahead. Think like your child. And slow way down.

The key to this venture is to talk to your kids about the time the trip will take, in terms they can understand. Expect their needs to be different than they are at home, especially with food. On trips, food isn't just nourishment. It's also a way of breaking up long stretches of boring mileage and stays at places more interesting to you than them. Transform these negatives into positives, with planned surprises, special treats, extra attention, and patience, patience, patience.

CARS

Traveling by car is an exciting way to see the countryside. You can stop when and wherever you want to sightsee, eat, or just relax, and take as much time as you like to get to your destination. While rolling along the highway with your child, share the scenery, sights, and sounds of the open road. Most of all be patient, and enjoy the ride!

En Route

When planning your car trip, know what travel times work for your kids. Some families prefer traveling at night because their children will sleep. Consider breaking the trip up into smaller parts as opposed to one marathon trip.

W e always take along hand puppets for long car or plane rides. When our kids are bored or cranky, we slip on the puppets, talk in funny voices, and the mood is broken. Sometimes the kids want to play with the

TRAVEL LOG

puppets themselves. Either way, our kids are happier and we've bought a little peace, with the help of Muff and Duff and a few other characters.

—*Mark L., Tustin, California*

Travel in comfortable clothes—loose, cotton clothing works best—and pack a small bag of back-up clothes that are easily accessible.

Don't travel at peak hours if any other option exists. Plan ahead, and listen to the radio for traffic reports around urban areas during rush hour.

The "Are We There Yet?" Syndrome

A two- or three-hour car trip may seem like a relatively short jaunt to you, but to toddlers and preschoolers especially, it's an eternity. Questions such as "Are we there yet?" or "When are we stopping?" may pop up frequently during long periods of inactivity or repetitive scenery. To engage your child and make moments such as these more enjoyable, plan plenty of diversions such as games, activities, snacks, coloring books, storybooks, books-on-tape, toys, and comfort objects (blankets, stuffed animals). Have these items easily accessible. (You can buy special toys that strap onto car seats for babies.) Choose items that are soft and light—sudden braking or an accident could turn a toy into a dangerous flying object.

Tote bag amusements

A tote bag filled with special surprises may keep your child intrigued for long periods, especially if you have enough different items to carry you through the trip. Plan for at least one item per hour. Let your kids pack their own bags with a few, travel-safe favorite items. Music and books-on-tape also engage children on the road. It's a myth that you need special children's music, even for babies. Young children may well enjoy the same music you do if you select sensitively (light classical, melodic pop, dance, reggae, world music). Kids like rhythm and positive energy, which gives you a wide range for mutual enjoyment. You can make your own books-on-tape by reading your kids' favorite stories onto cassettes.

TOY KIT CHECKLIST

- [ ] Balls
- [ ] Books-on-tape
- [ ] Coloring books
- [ ] Comfort items
- [ ] Drawing paper
- [ ] Road games
- [ ] Special new toys for the trip
- [ ] Storybooks
- [ ] Washable markers

I spy a . . .

Participatory games, singing, and storytelling are perhaps the best diversions for children because they involve the whole family. The game "I'm thinking of an animal," a good one for preschoolers, works like this: You or your child imagines an animal and the others in the vehicle ask clue-type questions such as "Is it a mammal/bird/reptile?" or "Does it have four legs or two?" You can also make up stories as a family, with everyone adding something in turn. Skill-building games in the car are a fun and educational way to pass the time. For example, your child can count cars of different colors or shout out numbers he reads on signs.

Test all games at home first to make sure your child enjoys them, then save them for your trip.

Tide you overs

Pair nutritious and not-too-messy when planning for snacks on the road. Good options include carrot sticks, raisins, or fresh or dried fruit. Juices boxes with straws minimize spills as do sippy cups with non-spill lids. Avoid red-colored juices that may stain car upholstery; serve white grape juice, apple juice, or sugar-free lemonade. If you're going to stop for a meal, involve your kids in the decision of where to eat, but be ready to stop soon after the decision is made or "Are we there yet?" may start up again in earnest.

Pit stops

Everyone travels better with occasional stops for leg-stretching and sightseeing. Especially, restless kids awaiting to arrive at their destination. To help make those long stretches on the road enjoyable, plan breaks every two hours or so and be flexible if your kids need more.

Look at breaks not just as a quick stop to stretch, but also as integral parts of your vacation. Picnic at a rest stop that has tables and a grassy area for running and playing (if you carry a ball, you can even get in a game of catch), or stop at a viewpoint or other scenic or fun spot. Do some research before you go. Find out if

What I look forward to almost more than anything on car trips is the chance to nap while my husband drives. Naps are a luxury I never get at home. But I want to be a good mom, too, and our son needs entertaining while we travel. So I figured out a solution that works like a charm. I make cassette tapes of myself reading my son's favorite stories, then I pop them in the tape player, and turn off the front speakers. That way, I can zone out in the front, Terrell gets his story in the back, and everyone's happy, even Roy, who likes to drive.

—*Kela J., Chapel Hill, North Carolina*

playgrounds, zoos, parks, or other scenic sights are along your route.

TIMING DRIVE TIME
Plan on your car trip with toddlers and preschoolers to take about a third longer than without them. With newborns, the same distance will take

twice as long. If making time is important, drive long stretches when your kids are sleepy, such as after big meals, but don't push past their limits. Anticipate their needs and stop well before their breaking point.

When traveling in summer, be sure to carry a windshield cover and park in the shade—overheated kids won't last much longer than overheated engines. If your kids are cranky from hunger, take your meal stops at restaurants with salad bars or buffets. This will not only satisfy their hunger, but the cooling environment provides immediate gratification. And remember, whenever a bathroom is available, make sure they use it. If you don't, you may have to make another stop a few miles down the road.

AIRPLANES

Traveling by plane is a fast and convenient option when traveling with children. Especially with babies, many times children sleep through the whole flight. For toddlers and preschools, airports are a source of fascination. They can watch planes take off and land, and you can walk with them around the terminal while you're waiting to board. Many airports are child-friendly and have special carpeted play areas with climbing structures.

When planning a long distance, consider whether a non-stop flight is too much of a marathon for your child. If you're not in a hurry, ask about connecting flights with layover time. This will give your child and you a chance to stretch out and relax a bit before the last leg of the flight.

O ur first family trip to Laguna Beach last year really improved when we figured out that our two-year-old daughter knew better than we did how to relax on vacation. Once we adjusted to her pattern (play, eat, sleep, play, eat, sleep, etc.) instead of trying to cram as much as we could into every day, everything fell into place. There was time to smell the roses and the sea breezes and we realized how silly it was to rush around on our time off.

TRAVEL LOG

—Karen T., Troy, Michigan

Departure and Arrival Times

When making flight arrangements, plan departure and arrival times according to your child's sleep schedule as best as you can. Plan to arrive at your destination or at the airport just before his bedtime if possible. You may want to travel during times when he is most likely to sleep if you think he won't travel well if awake. Keep in mind that the flight cancellations and delays can upset the best-laid plans. To minimize that risk, book first flights of the day and check if your flight is on time before you go to the airport.

If your child's sleep time isn't your major consideration, you may want to try flying at off-peak times when it's more likely that you'll have empty seats next to you. With more space, both you and your child will have more room to maneuver. Plus your child can move to another seat if he's restless. Your child's noise and antics will be less likely to bother other passengers on an uncrowded flight.

Seats for Little Ones

Airlines require children over a certain age—usually two—to have a paid seat. For children younger than two, the Federal Aviation Administration recommends that you fly with your child next to you in a car seat rather than on your lap. Many airlines sell discounted seats such as half-fares for children under two. Ask about these when making your reservations.

By purchasing a separate seat for your child, you're guaranteed a spot for his safety seat. Some airlines, however, permit parents to use an empty seat for free if they find one on board. As a result, some parents gamble on free children's seats by making reservations on flights that are not likely to be sold out. One strategy is to reserve a window seat and an aisle seat if there are three seats in the row. Few people reserve the middle seat, and airlines will assign all aisle and window seats first, so your odds of getting a seat increase. You may also find empty seats if you fly at off-peak times and off-peak seasons. You may even find people who are willing to switch seats to accommodate you.

If you are unable to get an unoccupied seat, however, you must keep your child on your lap, at risk to the child's safety (the flight attendant will send the car seat to the baggage compartment).

Choosing the right car seat

The Federal Aviation Administration (FAA) recommends that all children who fly use the restraint system appropriate for their height and weight. For children under 40 pounds, a car seat (also known as child restraint system or CRS) enhances child safety for both accidents and turbulence. Check to see if your car seat is certified for air travel.

Backless booster seats, safety belt extensions, and vest or harness devices that attach to an adult or to the seatbelt of the child's own seat are no longer permitted for use as child safety seats on airplanes. In the United States, supplemental lap restraints, or "belly belts," are also banned from use in both automobiles and aircraft. Some of these products may have been manufactured prior to the FAA ban on their use on aircraft and may still carry an FAA insignia. To find out if your car seat has been approved for use on airplanes, contact the FAA (see Resources section). Here are additional guidelines:

▶ Rear facing seat: for children under 20 pounds.
▶ Front-facing seat: for children from 20 to 40 pounds.
▶ Seat must usually be no wider than 16 inches to fit on airplane seat.
▶ Do not put child in seat designed for a smaller child.
▶ Shoulder straps must come out of the slots above your child's shoulders. To fit, adjust straps according to manufacturer's instructions.
▶ Place seat in window seat so it will not block the escape path in an emergency. Do not sit in an exit row. Request a different seat assignment instead.

- ▶ Fasten car seat to airplane seat as tightly as possible with seat belt. Ask for assistance if you are having trouble.
- ▶ Ask airline staff to assist you in making connections when traveling with children and a child safety seat.

Keep your child in the car seat for the entire flight. You never know when turbulence will hit. For more information on using car seats when flying, contact the Federal Aviation Administration (FAA) (see Family Resources section).

Where to Sit

With babies

Bulkhead seats (the ones up front near the cabin) provide more room for families with babies to move and, for breastfeeding moms, a little more privacy. You will, however, have to stash all your carry-on luggage in overhead compartments because you won't usually have storage room under the seat in front of you. Therefore, keep necessities near the front of the compartment. Fortunately, families with babies always board before other passengers, enabling you to utilize compartments above your seats.

With toddlers and preschoolers

Kids often choose window seats if asked, but aisle seats are a better option because they allow kids to step out a bit. Some families prefer the bulkhead because of the extra leg room. Keep in mind, though, that these seats have fixed armrests, which won't allow your kids to rest on your lap when they get tired.

Getting to the Gate

A cardinal rule when getting to the airport is to allow lots of extra time for bathroom stops, diaper changes, nursing, and other schedule challenges. Remember you're on kid time now and you'll want the pre-flight process to be as unhurried and un-harried as possible, for your kids' sake as much as yours.

With babies

Expect the unexpected—the diaper change that can't wait—allow for it in your planning, and accept it when it happens.

With toddlers and preschoolers

To make those morning flights, let kids fly in their pajamas or put them to bed in comfy travel clothes the night before.

On-Board Diaper Changing

Bring sufficient disposable diapers, wipes (in a resealable plastic bag to keep them moist), and changes of clothing (including clothing for you) on-board for one change per-hour of flight. Bring plastic bags for soiled diapers and clothes. For baby's clothes, separates work better than one-piece outfits. When something gets soiled, it's easier to change a shirt or pair of shorts than a whole outfit. You'll need to pack fewer clothes that way, too, and you'll buy more time between Laundromat trips. Pack some waterless antibacterial gels to help you clean your hands after changes.

Cabin Fever

Being belted in for hours on an airplane can be even more trying for your child than long car rides, because pit stops are not an option. As with car travel, be prepared with plenty of distractions, including stories to tell, paperback picture books (lighter and less bulky to carry), special games and toys (select small, light ones), paper and washable markers for drawing, and special foods.

Special and surprise are key here. If certain playthings, foods, and activities are reserved for travel only, your child may look forward to them and that will help pass the time much better than familiar things. Remember to test travel toys, foods, and games in advance so you know your kids enjoy them.

Time Zones and Jet Lag

Jet lag and other shocks to the body's clock are hard enough on adults; imagine what they do to kids, and to us when we travel with them. Fortunately, you can take several steps to minimize the problems. Before your departure date, alter your child's schedule so that it's closer to what it will be on the road. Going west to east? Over a three-day span, bump bedtime and wake-up time back a little bit more each day. Do the reverse if going east to west.

When you arrive at your destination, get some sun. Local sunlight helps reset the body's clock and eases jet lag. Don't plan too many activities for the first two days. If you're going to spend a week or more in a new time zone, put your kids on the local schedule beforehand to prepare. If the time change will exceed seven hours, try to schedule nighttime flights. Yes, your kids may have a hard time sleeping en route and that's the idea. Once you get where you're going, your exhausted little ones will be more likely to fall asleep when night falls. A good night's sleep—and a semi-regular routine—are important. Overtired kids are one of the biggest threats to an enjoyable family vacation.

TRAINS

A train ride may be the most family-friendly form of travel on the planet, at least for moderate distances. With no cramped quarters or seat-belt imprisonment like planes or cars, kids can get up and move around. The scenery is much better at track-level than at 30,000 feet in the air. Other advantages include on-board bathrooms, drinking fountains, and snacks to buy. Add in affordable fares and the option to purchase sleeping berths and you have a travel adventure that may become one of your family's fondest memories.

5

Dining à la Kid

FOR MANY, EXPERIENCING a mouthwatering marathon of exotic meals in faraway places is a vacation unto itself. And with a little ingenuity and foresight, you can even share those gastronomically satisfying journeys with a child in tow. The key is satisfying your child's needs before moving on to your own preferences. The compromise may be as simple as preparing a simple cheese sandwich in the hotel room for your three-year-old before heading off to try a new restaurant, or making reservations at a time when your infant is likely to fall asleep.

Dining out isn't the only option. If you want to take a break from the selections that exist outside, take advantage of the meal options inside. Below you'll find tips on how to eat well in your hotel room and how to take advantage of your kitchenette without sacrificing your vacation to do it.

EATING IN
When You Have a Kitchen

Kitchens can be a real blessing when traveling with kids. Kitchens enable you to have food on hand when your hungry child's tiny tummy needs nourishment. Kitchens also help cut the cost of travel. Going out every night for a meal adds up in a hurry, especially in expensive destination such as New York, Rome, or Tokyo. Cooking family meals in your suite may not be the ideal way to relax on the road, but it can be the economical difference that makes your trip possible in the first place.

This doesn't mean you have to burn away all your vacation time in front of a hot stove. Unless you love cooking, start by resolving yourself of not spending long hours planning and cooking meals. Instead, plan simple meals that don't require a lot of time to prepare. You can also buy prepared foods at local markets that may only need to be heated either in an oven or microwave. Think of your kitchen-away-from-home as not only as economical advantage but as a way to enjoy your accommodations and share some quality time with your child.

Y ou never know how far you'll need to go to find a decent market when you stay at a hotel. So when we take a car trip with our family, we always stop at the first acceptable-looking grocery store we see, once we've entered

TRAVEL LOG

the town where we'll be staying. That way, we arrive at our room

fully stocked up for our kids. Then we can just unpack and stay put for awhile. There's plenty to do to settle down kids at a new place without having to go grocery shopping on top of it!

—Tania D., Fort Collins, Colorado

Planning Your Indoor Picnic

The days have long past when eating in a hotel room meant dining on crackers and cheese. Between markets, food stands, and take-out places, you can find a wide array of savory and nutritious ready-to-eat entrees, salads, sandwiches, side dishes, and desserts to satisfy almost every taste.

Neighborhood supermarkets are always a good option for all sorts of ready-to-eat or easy-to-prepare foods. Natural food stores, an alternative to supermarkets, stock high quality breads, prepared foods, yogurts, cheeseless pizzas, tofu, and produce, which are healthier but can be a bit more expensive. You will also find many naturally sweetened breakfast cereals and granolas far healthier than the sugar-laden choices found in chain supermarkets. Many large supermarkets carry some of these items as well, in special natural foods sections.

If you're staying in a large city, you may also want to check out local delicatessens, which serve a variety of ready-to-eat items such as hot and cold entrees and sandwiches, potato salad, hummus, and bean salad.

Lastly, check out the take-out and delivery options in the area you're staying in. Pizza and Chinese are fairly common and good family dinner options. Many hotels provide menus of nearby restaurants that offer take-out or delivery.

Ready-to-eat items often come with plastic forks, knives, or spoons and paper napkins. You can also buy small packages of plastic, washable picnic plates, cups, and utensils at the same supermarket you buy your food.

TRAVEL LOG

We used to make picnic lunches on vacations instead of going to restaurants because it was easier with the kids. We've since learned that going to parks with a picnic lunch is a great way to get a feel for new place, so we actually prefer it to going out to eat. We buy our food at food stands or in markets so we're not spending any effort to prepare the picnic. Plus the kids can run around afterward, which makes their mood better for the rest of the day and helps them sleep better, too.

—*Paula Y., Tacoma, Washington*

HOTEL ROOM UTENSILS

Hold on to those plastic utensils you get at food stands, take-out restaurants, and supermarket delis if you didn't bring any from home. Wrap them in a napkin to be washed and reused later.

Outdoor Picnics

If you don't have a kitchenette, you can break up the restaurant routine with a picnic at a pretty spot or place where your kids can run and play. Like an indoor picnic, you can buy ready-to-eat meals at supermarkets, food stands and delis, or order take-out and head to the nearest park or green area. Hotel staff may be able to recommend good choices where you can go outside to eat without going out to eat.

Nutritious, Low-Maintenance Meals

It's hard to maintain a healthy diet when traveling, especially if you eat out most of the time. Restaurant food tends to be high in both fat and sugar. If you plan on dining in, the following are some nutritious, easy-to-manage options:

▶ Buy a large, long loaf of whole-grain bread and make a giant sub for the family with different sections for members with different tastes.

- Buy pita bread and fillings—vegetables, cheeses, hummus, and low-fat meats such as skinned turkey or chicken.
- Homemade, gourmet pizzas can be quite healthy if you avoid high-fat items such as cheese and pepperoni. Buy prepared pizza crusts and pile on healthier items such as artichoke hearts, mushrooms, peppers, tomatoes, and skinned chicken. Use modest amounts of cheese—low-fat varieties such as mozzarella or provolone.
- Buy large tortillas for burritos and fill with beans, veggies, olives, lettuce, guacamole, and a smattering of cheese. You can also add lean meats such as skinned, diced chicken.
- Cook a pot of pasta and mix with bottled sauce.
- Buy nutritious microwaveable frozen foods such as manicotti, pocket sandwiches, Asian foods, and other entrees that are low in fat, sugar, and sodium. Read the item's label for this information.

BRINGING FOOD FROM HOME
PROS:
- The familiarity of something prepared by parents is often comforting to young children.
- You'll save time and money by not having to go out as often.
- Kids get hungry much more often than adults, so having food they like at hand is a good idea.

CONS:

▶ Food is heavy and bulky, and the containers you bring it in, such as a cooler and cold packs, substantially add to its weight and bulk.

▶ Food not eaten is susceptible to spoiling or going stale.

COPING WITH EATING PROBLEMS

When kids don't eat well on trips, any number of factors may be at play. Here are some of the most common eating problems, along with what to do about them:

Unfamiliarity

Kids are not always as adventurous as adults when exploring new foods in new places. If only new foods are available and your child resists them, encourage her to try a mouthful or create a game of trying the new foods, such as wandering around the Southwestern states doing a taste-test of local chilies.

Timing

Toddlers eat widely varying amounts from day to day, so don't be alarmed if your toddler doesn't have much of an appetite during a certain mealtime. Kids don't have the same concept as adults do about what foods should be eaten when. If your child doesn't want to eat much for breakfast, she may eat more for dinner or lunch.

Individuality

By preschool age, kids have a pretty clear idea of what they like. It's also important for them to assert their preferences by this age. Therefore, you may find it difficult to convince a child of this age to eat something she says she doesn't want. One way you can work with your child is to try a compromise. For example, if you're going out for lunch and your child wants some cereal in the room first, let her have a little and tell her she can have more after lunch. That way, she knows you've respected her choice, and you know she'll be at least somewhat hungry at the restaurant.

DINING OUT: BEST-BET RESTAURANTS

Often the first thought that comes to mind when dining out with children is where to find the nearest family-style restaurant. You'll be glad to know that although you will have to alter the way you pick restaurants, your options are not as limited as you may think. Instead of family-style, think family-friendly.

When choosing a family-friendly restaurant, seek out places with a casual atmosphere such as pizza, Mexican, and American restaurants. Many casual restaurants serve a variety of entrees, and in generous portions. In addition, noisy kids fit right in with the energetic chat. Ask about highchair and booster seat availability, and even activities for kids (such as crayons and place mats that have pictures to color). The menu may have a children's section—or better yet, a separate children's version—with several simple, inexpensive selections (peanut butter and jelly, melted cheese, spaghetti, for example.) Tables are usually widely spaced so kids can wander between them without

HOW TO SIZE UP A CHILD-FRIENDLY RESTAURANT

☐ Friendly, welcoming staff

☐ Casual atmosphere

☐ Highchairs and booster seats

☐ Activities for children such as crayons and small coloring books or place mats to be colored

☐ Tables widely spaced to make way for wandering children

☐ Children's menu, or section in main menu with children's items

☐ Rapid service

☐ Lots of other families as patrons

disturbing other patrons. Service is generally fast and friendly.

You'll want to avoid quiet, romantic, formal restaurants. The patrons and ownership of such places may look askance at noisy children or babies and the kitchens aren't likely to cater to children's simple tastes.

What kids will eat in a restaurant depends on what they eat at home. If they've been exposed to, and liked, some exotic choices at home, they're more likely to be open to new foods in restaurants. Otherwise, your family vacation may not be the best time to try Korean food, for example, unless the menu includes simple items that are popular with kids.

The following tips will help make your family dining-out experience a success:

For babies
▶ Feed baby first so you will be free to eat your food when it arrives. Alternatively, time going out when you know baby is likely to sleep.
▶ Sit near the door so you can rush outside with your baby if she cries. You want to be considerate of other patrons and you don't want to make the proprietor or manager anxious.
▶ Bring a bib.

For toddlers and preschoolers

▶ If your child is noisy or unusually active, go out for breakfast or lunch instead of dinner. Restaurant atmosphere is more relaxed at those times.

▶ Bring snacks for your kids in case you have to wait awhile before being seated or served. Snacks also help when your kids don't like what is ordered for them. Foods that take awhile to eat will make a wait more tolerable for everyone. Bring boxes of raisins: they're compact and self-contained, they take a long time to pick out of the box, and they're nutritious and filling enough to satisfy a hungry child.

▶ Order side orders for your kids to keep them happy while the main orders are being prepared.

▶ Have small toys, games, stickers, or an old purse filled with surprises for an active child to do in case she's not hungry. Make sure any toys or games you bring are quiet ones. Newer toys and games will likely occupy her longer than familiar ones.

▶ With an active child, you may want to stroll either around the restaurant or outside after ordering. Remember to alert the waiter that you're going.

▶ Request that your child's food arrives when yours does so you have more time to eat your own meal.

▶ Let your child try your meal, which may make her feel special and help her look forward to the next time you go out.

For all young children

▶ Ask for a booth if available.

▶ Go early or late to minimize disturbances of other patrons, especially in places that don't cater to families.

▶ You may want to carry a drop cloth to put under a highchair or in front of a toddler in case of a mess.

▶ Never change a child's diapers at the table.

▶ Tip well. Even if your child doesn't cause problems or make a mess, any extra attention they receive should be rewarded.

▶ If your kids are cranky before you go out, you may want to change or delay your plans.

IT'S A SMALL WORLD— MENU CHOICES

The following international specialties are mild-tasting enough for young children:

▶ **Greek—spanakopita (spinach and cheese in a pastry shell)**

▶ **Italian—manicotti or cheese ravioli with marinara sauce**

▶ **Thai/Chinese/Vietnamese—mild vegetable dumplings or noodle soups**

▶ **Japanese—tempura or teriyaki vegetables (colorful and sweet)**

▶ **Mexican—quesadillas (cheese melted on tortillas) or mild cheese enchiladas**

▶ **Jewish—cheese blintzes (sweet and fun to unwrap)**

EATING ELSEWHERE
Trains

When it comes to meals on the move, trains far surpass eating in cars and on planes. You've got room to maneuver for serving and cleaning up, or you can eat at a table in the dining car. Like restaurants, though, be sure the dining car selections will satisfy your kids or that they'll like whatever snacks are available on the train. Just in case, bring enough of your child's favorite non-perishable foods to get them through the journey.

Note, too, that although train rides are relatively smooth, you should keep cups and bowls no more than two-thirds full at any time. Similar precautions are taken in the dining car as well.

HEALTHY SNACKS TO GO

- ☐ Apple slices
- ☐ Healthy cookies and crackers (avoid hydrogenated or partially hydrogenated oils)
- ☐ Raisins or other dried fruit
- ☐ Carrot sticks
- ☐ String cheese
- ☐ Juice in boxes with straws

Planes

Airlines today are serving meals on fewer and fewer flights, especially shorter flights, in an effort to reduce cost. Portion sizes are small, and the limited selections may not be to your family's liking. Most airlines, however, provide special meals such as children's selections, low-fat/low-cholesterol, gluten-free, vegan, vegetarian, diabetic, low-sodium, and kosher. Although you can request these meals 24 hours before your flight, it's best to order them when you make your reservations (confirm your choice at least 24 hours before, however, to prevent mix-ups). Be sure to request meals that are appropriate for your child, but carry on food in case you need it.

In many airports, you will find a wide variety of foods at food carts in the gate areas. The food is packed for carrying on, with utensils, condiments, and napkins included.

When eating on a plane, trade off with your partner so one of you can tend to your child while the other eats. Avoid drinking hot tea or coffee when traveling with your child. Turbulence can happen at any time and cause you to spill the scalding liquid on him.

While in town for business, my husband and I were staying in a hotel in San Francisco with our two children. We knew San Francisco was a great town for ethnic food but didn't know where to go. In a local alternative

TRAVEL LOG

press publication that had restaurant reviews, we spotted a Middle Eastern place nearby that sounded interesting so we packed up Janie and Caleb and headed over there. The place looked like a real hole in the wall, but it was clean so we ventured in. What a delight! The owner was this grandmotherly type from Iran who cooked and served the food herself. There were two tables inside and all that separated us from the kitchen was a counter with the cash register and menus on top. It was like eating in someone's breakfast nook. Very intimate and informal, and she was wonderful to the children. Plus, the food was marvelous, as if she prepared it for very special guests. Now whenever we travel to American cities, we go to a major bookstore and pick up a copy of the local alternative press paper (which is always free). Generally, there will be a section with capsule reviews of local restaurants including many interesting choices like my favorite hole-in-the-wall in San Francisco.

—*Kelly B., Madison, Wisconsin*

6

All Abroad

YOU CAN HAVE THE MOST memorable adventures when traveling out of the country with young children. The basic planning strategies for traveling with children anywhere apply, but you'll need to add a few steps when traveling abroad. This chapter will help you prepare for your out-of-country experience, with sections on passports and immunizations, what to bring, transportation, and meals.

PASSPORTS

You and each of your children will need passports to depart or enter the United States and to enter and depart most foreign countries. Exceptions include short-term travel between the United States and Mexico, Canada, and some countries in the Caribbean, where a U.S. birth certificate or other proof of U.S. citizenship may be accepted. Even newborn babies need their own passports to travel. Your child's passport is good for five years. Adult passports are valid for 10 years.

Even if you are not required to have a passport to visit a foreign country, U.S. Immigration requires you to prove your U.S. citizenship and identity to re-enter the United States. Make certain that you carry adequate documentation to pass through U.S. Immigration upon your return. However, a U.S. passport is still the best proof of U.S. citizenship.

Your travel agent or airline can tell you if you need a passport for the country that you plan to visit. You can also find this information from the Federal Consumer Information Center (see Family Resources section).

London took on totally new dimensions when we were with the children. Where Steve and I would have nixed the double-decker bus tours as too hokey, the kids talked us into it. We were glad they did. The narrative showed

TRAVEL LOG

us some things we might have otherwise missed, and the kids just reveled in seeing the sights from the open-air top of the bus. (Hint: Dress warmly or save this for a relatively balmy day.) In Trafalgar Square, we didn't simply marvel at the pigeons—we took the time to feed them. Even simple things, such as a taxi ride, took on added notoriety when my children pointed out that the cabs were "Chitty Chitty Bang Bang" cars (they were what we would typically consider old-fashioned autos).

—*Bonnie S., Honolulu, Hawaii*

Applying for Your Passport

Apply for your passport several months in advance of your planned departure. You can apply for a passport at many Federal and state courts, probate courts, some county/municipal offices, and some post offices.

Children under 13 do not need to appear in person for the passport application process, but a parent or legal guardian must appear on the child's behalf. You will need to go to a courthouse, county/municipal office, or post office authorized to accept passport applications and complete the DSP-11 passport application form. This form is also available from the U.S. State Department Web site. (See Family Resources section.)

When applying for passports for both yourself and your children, you are required to bring the following:

Proof of citizenship

A previous U.S. passport or a certified copy of your U.S. birth certificate issued by the state, city, or county of your birth (a certified copy will have a registrar's embossed seal and the date the certificate was filed with the registrar's office) will validate your citizenship. If you or your child were born abroad, you must present a Certificate of Naturalization, Certificate of Citizenship, Report of Birth Abroad of a U.S. Citizen,

PASSPORT APPLICATION CHECKLIST:

☐ Proof of U.S. citizenship
☐ Photographs
☐ Proof of identity
☐ Fees
☐ Social Security number

or a Certification of Birth (Form FS-545 or DS-1350). If you do not have these documents, check with the passport acceptance agent for documents that can be used in their place.

Photographs

For each passport you must submit two identical photographs (taken within the past six months) in either color or black and white. Photographs must be 2x2 inches in size, showing a front view, full face, on white or off-white background. In many cities, you will find photography shops within blocks of the passport office that will quickly develop passport photos. Otherwise, consult your yellow pages for photography studios that take passport photos.

Bring extra passport photographs along with a photocopy of the passport information pages for each family member. Keep the extras separate from the passports and leave an extra set at home. In the event your passports are lost or stolen, this will enable you to replace them easier.

Proof of identity

The following items are generally acceptable documents of identity for passport applications if they contain your signature and if they readily identify you by physical description or photograph:

- ► A previous U.S. passport
- ► A Certificate of Naturalization or Citizenship
- ► A valid driver's license
- ► A government-issued (Federal, state, municipal) identification card

Fees

Passport fees are $60 for an adult age 16 and over and $40 for children under 16. This includes a $15 execution fee for applying in person. If you must have your passport in less than 25 business days, you must pay an additional $35 expedite fee to ensure urgent handling.

Social Security number

If you do not provide a Social Security number, you must pay the Internal Revenue Service a $500 fee.

Important Passport Changes Afoot

With the number of international child custody cases on the rise, single parents traveling with underage children have often been detained or prevented from boarding planes, and from entering Canada, Mexico and several South American countries. Several countries have instituted passport requirements to help prevent child abductions. Mexico, for example, requires a child traveling alone or with only one parent or in someone else's custody to carry written, notarized consent from the absent parent or parents. No authorization is needed if the child travels alone and is in possession of a U.S. passport. A child traveling alone with a birth certificate requires written, notarized authorization from both parents.

U.S. policy will soon require the signature of both parents on a child's passport application. Check with your local passport office before applying to find out if both parents must appear in person or if notarized signatures of both parents on the application will suffice. To avoid problems, parents traveling alone with children should also bring notarized letters from both parents authorizing the international travel of the children.

I t sounds ambitious, but we've found that overseas vacations work great with our young family (one toddler, one preschooler, and one preteen). Ireland is an especially good fit with young children. Places like Bunratty

TRAVEL LOG

Castle, with its medieval banquet and entertainment, really appeal to toddlers and preschoolers as well as older kids (there are no utensils, even adults wear bibs, and they actually encourage you to be noisy at meal time). There are ruined castles to explore, inexpensive farmhouses where small children are not only welcome but doted upon, and a quieter, slower pace that matches kids' own sense of time. Even the local pubs—at least in the countryside— are family-friendly. The ones we went to had board games and crayons, which made for an affordable, entertaining evening out for all concerned.

—*Molly B., Austin, Texas*

WHAT TO BRING

The little things matter most when you're traveling with your children in a foreign country. As much as you can, think about where it is you'll be and try to anticipate what items will or won't be available when you get there. Your child may settle down more easily in a strange environment if a few of the comforts of home are handy. Think about the everyday conveniences such as Band-Aids, disposable diapers, dry cereals— and pack a supply for the length of your stay.

Disposable Diapers

Pack a full supply of disposable diapers for your vacation in a sturdy cardboard box that you can check at the airport. You'll find this more convenient than trying to find your favorite brand of diapers abroad. Put your name on the inside and outside of the box and mark with brightly colored tape so it's instantly recognizable on the baggage carousel. Be sure to include a separate supply of diapers for your travel time in your carry-on luggage.

If you do have to buy extras in a foreign country, know your baby's weight in kilos before you leave home. The sizes (in weight) printed on the packages will be in kilos not pounds.

Infant Formula and Bottles

Bring prepared bottles of formula or milk to be refrigerated by the flight attendant for use on the plane. Bring formula in ready-to-use cans, along with a supply of disposable, pre-sterilized bottles and nipples for the remainder of your trip. Consider shipping a supply of formula with the box of diapers. Include enough for travel time in your carry-on luggage.

Baby Food

Favorite baby foods go a long way toward making your dining experiences abroad more relaxed. Unopened jars of baby food do not need to be refrigerated, and are good to have on hand as insurance, no matter where you're traveling.

Flashlight

Pack a small battery-operated flashlight or portable nightlight if your child needs light to fall asleep at night. Hotel rooms in foreign countries may not have nightlights or even street lamps shining in through the windows. A flashlight will also help everyone navigate the unfamiliar path to the bathroom in a pitch dark hotel room.

ID YOUR CHILD

Your child should always carry identification and contact numbers. Write your child's name, your name, hotel address and phone number, and the

phone numbers of contacts back home on a business or index card. Tuck this inside a zippered pocket on your child's coat or inside his shoe.

Prescriptions

Pack your child's prescription medicines in the original containers with legible ingredients and instructions. Make sure the country to which you are traveling has no restrictions on the drugs you're carrying. For preexisting conditions, bring a signed letter from your child's doctor that describes the condition and gives the generic and brand names of the prescribed drugs. For

HANDY TO HAVE

These items are not always readily available in foreign lands, so bring some along:

- ☐ Liquid Castile soap for bathing and shampooing
- ☐ Powdered laundry soap in travel-sized packs
- ☐ Small can of stain remover
- ☐ Clothes pins
- ☐ Resealable plastic bags in large and small sizes
- ☐ Tissues in travel packs or an extra roll of toilet paper
- ☐ Plastic trash bags

more information, contact the Centers for Disease Control and Prevention (see Family Resources section). Also, contact the country's embassy for customs regulations relating to prescription medicines. Pack all medicines in carry-on luggage, and keep your medical insurance information and pediatrician's telephone numbers easily accessible.

PUBLIC TRANSPORTATION

Public transportation, especially in Europe and England, is a convenient and economical way to get around. If you're planning on using public transportation, however, first consider the safety factor. Although many countries have taxis, rental cars, and buses, some vehicles are not equipped with seat belts, which also rules out using car seat for your baby.

Trains

Train travel in many countries can be an enjoyable and pleasant way to take in the scenery. You'll not only save money by not renting a car but you'll also save money when traveling as a family. Children under 12 travel for half price and those under four travel for free. With a Eurailpass, you can travel easily in first- or second-class to Austria, Belgium, Denmark, Finland, France,

Germany, Greece, Holland, Hungary, Ireland, Italy, Luxembourg, Norway, Portugal, Spain, Sweden, and Switzerland. Your travel agent can help you purchase a Eurailpass, which entitles you to as many trips and destinations between these countries as the time limit on your pass allows. If you are traveling in England, Scotland, and Wales, look into a BritRail pass (see Family Resources section).

Ask your travel agent about other discounts for family travel or special children's programs on rail companies. You might also ask about any unusual train customs in the country to which you are traveling. In Slovakia, children under 12 or under five feet must ride in the back of the train. On Romanian trains, children are

TRAIN TIPS

☐ Ask for a nonsmoking car.

☐ Board as early as possible to find a good seat—look for a four-seater that will allow you to spread out a bit.

☐ Bring infant and child-care items.

☐ Bring baby food, bread, fruit, and cheese or other snacks.

☐ Carry only the amount of luggage you can manage yourself.

☐ Play "I Spy" games with your child.

expected to sit on their parents' laps unless an empty seat is available.

When traveling by train with children, consider traveling first class for the additional space. You can also request a family space in second class when you make reservations.

Buses

While bus travel is easily the most budget-friendly mode of transportation, carefully consider if it is appropriate for your family. Buses make frequent stops and seating arrangements are confined. With no room to roam around, your toddler or preschooler is likely to be a challenge on board.

If you are traveling with an infant, bring everything you need to care for the child in a diaper bag or backpack. You may also want to bring a soft carrier, since you will be holding your baby for the entire trip.

If you're traveling with a toddler or preschooler, choose a seat in the front of the bus if available, so your child will have a better view out the windows. Bring snacks along with amusements for the ride—stickers, coloring book, small cars, dolls, or action figures. Consider letting your child pack and carry his own child-sized backpack of snacks and toys.

Subways

Subways systems are an efficient way to move from one locale to another when sightseeing in large cities. Traveling underground, they move through the city with ease, enabling you to cover a lot of ground quicker and easier than by car or bus. But subways can be a stressful place when traveling with children. Most escalators do not accommodate strollers, and you may have to wait in line for tokens in busy stations or read a map in a foreign language—all with a child in tow.

Before you head out on a sightseeing excursion, plan ahead. Get a subway or metro map in advance of your sightseeing day and plan your entry and departure points beforehand. Ask your hotel personnel about planned subway stops and itinerary. They may also be able to advise you about particular stations and the best times of day to travel with children.

RENTING A CAR

When renting a car for your family abroad, make arrangements beforehand with the help of a travel agent. If you reserve and prepay in U.S. dollars, you can avoid unexpected rate changes and currency fluctuations. Ask for a confirmation of your reservation in writing and get a voucher detailing whether unlimited mileage is included, double-digit value-added taxes are paid, and the pickup and drop-off times. Confirm the size of the car as well, because car labels such as mid-sized or family sedan do not necessarily mean the same thing abroad.

Car Seats

Let your travel agent know that you will be bringing your own child safety restraint or car seat. Have your travel agent confirm that the rear seats of your rental car will have seat belts and that those seat belts will accommodate a child's car seat. Many car rental agencies abroad do not have car seats for rent at all or do not allow one-way rental of seats. Avis, Hertz, Budget and National car rental companies rent car seats in some foreign cities, but one-way rentals may not be available. If you need to reserve a car seat, confirm it with your agent and car rental company in advance and in writing when you reserve your car.

Insurance and Permits

Check your credit cards and your own auto insurer to see if you're covered for damage and liability, and buy coverage from the rental companies if you're not (it costs $12-$25 per day). Foreign car rental agencies usually provide auto insurance, but in some countries the required coverage is minimal. When renting a car abroad, consider purchasing insurance coverage that is at least equivalent to your coverage at home.

You may also want to get an international driving permit through the American Automobile Association (AAA) or American Automobile Touring Alliance (AATA). International driving permits do not replace standard driver's licenses; they are only supplements to valid licenses. Contact the AAA or AATA to find out which countries require international driving permits.

Safety

In many places frequented by tourists, including areas of southern Europe, victimization of tourists in rental cars is quite common. Where it is a problem, U.S. embassies and consular officers work with local authorities to warn the public about the dangers. In some locations, these efforts at public awareness have paid off, reducing the frequency of incidents.

When you rent a car, choose a type commonly available locally. Ask to have the rental car company identification removed from the car. You may also ask your rental car agency for advice on avoiding robbery while visiting tourist destinations. Don't leave your car unattended in gas stations or highway rest stops near airports. Never leave children unattended in a car under any circumstances (see Family Resources section for information about road security in other countries).

HAPPY MEALS

Dining with young children is an adventure no matter where you are. In a foreign land, a little extra attention, forethought, and flexibility will see you through. Have familiar and healthy foods available in your room such as cold cereal, peanut butter, crackers, and fresh fruit that can be washed and peeled.

When eating in restaurants, plan to go early, and look for places with menus in English to improve your odds of success with the menu. Order promptly and bring a small toy or crayons and coloring book.

With babies

If you're breastfeeding your baby, you may find you're more relaxed doing so in public places in other countries than you are here at home. If not, go for ready-to-use formula and use sealed, bottled water when mixing instant cereals and formula. In restaurants, bring a thermos and ask waiter or waitress to fill it for you with boiling water for mixing cereal.

TIPS FOR TODDLERS AND PRESCHOOLERS

☐ Have familiar snacks on hand to feed your child.

☐ Encourage your child to try simple local specialties.

☐ Avoid fruit shakes prepared by street vendors.

☐ Encourage your child to drink a lot of water (bottled is preferable).

With toddlers

Finger foods are good bets for older toddlers, and it's a good idea to have snacks handy for him throughout the day and wherever you go. Frequent grazing on

---

TRAVEL LOG

Our daughter was four when our family went to Provence. For much of the vacation, we were in a house with friends, so feeding our daughter was not a problem. We found cocoa crisp cereal in the local market, along with fresh fruits and pasta. On the weekend, though, my husband and I looked forward to some restaurant dining as we'd moved to a small hotel in Aix. Highlights for our daughter were the local Vietnamese restaurant, complete with tableside goldfish pond (the waiter brought our daughter food to feed the fish) and the creperie that offered simple fillings for her (ham, cheese, and strawberries for dessert) and ratatouille for us.

—*Lisa S., Portland, Maine*

---

familiar snacks should keep your child happy and make mealtimes less stressful, particularly if unfamiliar foods are on the menu. Plan to eat early with toddlers if possible. Full-service restaurants in many countries often do not serve dinner before 7 PM. If your child normally eats dinner at 6 PM, use snacks to tide him over or eat in cafés and pizzerias.

With preschoolers

Preparing your preschooler for the adventure of foods in a foreign country can be part of the fun you have together on your trip. The idea that you can have pizza or pasta every day in Italy should work wonders on just about any three-year-old. However, a hot dog in France served on a baguette with spicy mustard might just be the thing to convince your child to try something a bit more exotic. If you feel the need, you will find American alternative to ethnic food, like McDonald's or Pizza Hut in most countries. Your preschooler may also enjoy spotting the familiar outposts.

SAFE NOT SORRY

Any raw food could be contaminated, particularly in areas of poor sanitation. Foods of particular concern include salads, uncooked vegetables and fruit, unpasteurized milk and milk products, raw meat, and shellfish. Fruit, especially, may have been grown with contaminated irrigation water or sprayed with pesticides banned in developed nations. If you peel fruit yourself, it is generally safe. Food that has been cooked and is still hot is also generally safe. Warm or room temperature food can be a breeding ground for bacteria.

Some fish may be unsafe even when cooked because of the presence of toxins in their flesh. Toxins may show up in tropical reef fish, red snapper, amber jack, grouper, and sea bass at unpredictable times if caught on tropical reefs rather than in open ocean. The barracuda and puffer fish are often toxic and should generally be avoided. Highest risk areas include the islands of the West Indies, and the tropical Pacific and Indian Oceans. Go to the Centers for Disease Control and Prevention Web site (see Family Resources section) for information about food precautions in specific destinations.

DON'T DRINK THE WATER?

Contaminated water is a major source of intestinal illness in travelers of any age, especially children. Take special precautions to ensure drinking water is safe. When traveling with young children to the Caribbean or Mexico, or to other areas in Latin America, Asia, and Africa with poor sanitation, don't drink the local tap water. Even in countries where the water is fit for drinking, the youngest travelers may have trouble digesting unfamiliar minerals that might be present in the water. Most European cities have safe drinking water (especially at hotels and restaurants that cater to American tourists), but avoid unchlorinated tap water in rural areas or small villages as a precaution.

Check with your travel agent or the Centers for Disease Control and Prevention (see Family Resources section) for specific destinations and water advisories. In some areas, only the following beverages may be safe to drink' boiled water, hot beverages (such as coffee or tea) made with boiled water, canned or bottled carbonated beverages, beer, and wine. Ice may be made from unsafe water and should also be avoided. It is safer to drink from a can or bottle of beverage than to drink from a container that was not known to be clean and dry. Keep in mind that water on the surface of a can or bottle may also be contaminated, so clean the area that will touch your mouth, preferably with an antiseptic wipe, before drinking.

Boiling is the most reliable method to make water in certain areas safe for drinking. Bring water to a vigorous boil for one minute, then allow it to cool to room temperature naturally, without adding ice. At altitudes higher than 6,562 feet (2 km), boil for three minutes. To improve the water's taste after boiling, add a pinch of salt to each quart or pour the water several times from

WATER WISE

- ☐ Watch toddlers in the bath carefully to make sure they are not ingesting the water or getting it in their eyes.

- ☐ Ask your hotel about swimming pool maintenance and chlorination before letting your child swim; have your child wear goggles underwater.

- ☐ Wash and peel and fruits and vegetables before letting your child eat them. Avoid raw fruits and vegetables in questionable areas.

- ☐ Use sealed bottled water or boiled water for mixing formula or bring ready-to-use formula.

one container to another. If boiling isn't feasible, you can chemically disinfect the water with iodine but water should sit for 15 hours after treatment to make sure all bacteria are killed. Do not use chemically disinfected water for more than a few weeks at a time. You can buy iodine pills for this purpose at pharmacies and sporting goods stores. Follow manufacturer's instructions.

WHEN IN ROME . . .

Immerse yourself and your children in local customs and routines when appropriate and fun. Be open-minded. In Spain, for example, children are expected to go with their parents everywhere and they do not necessarily adhere to early bedtimes. You may see children playing out in the town square until midnight, and if your own children are up for some late night frolicking with the locals in the park, feel free to join in. Fine restaurants in places such as France generally do not welcome children, as dining is considered an adult pastime. Look to more relaxed dining in bistros, cafés, or bars. Teach your preschoolers a few simple phrases in the language of the country you are visiting. "Please," and "Thank you," in the native language may endear your family to the people you encounter and be a point of pride for your children as well.

"What's a bidet?" and similar questions and customs may not be as easily adapted or explained, however. Prepare your child in advance as much as possible for something as unusual as an in-ground toilet or the lack of toilet paper in restrooms. Use new and unfamiliar customs and circumstances as an opportunity for fun and learning together.

7

While You're There

THERE'S A LOT TO THINK ABOUT as you set out on a family vacation. Every family has its own likes and dislikes, and it goes without saying that you'll consider yours as you put your trip together. Keeping the cardinal rules of the road in the back of your head will also stand you in good stead.

TOP **TIPS**
Adjust Your Attitude

The moment you welcome a baby into your life, there's scarcely an hour that's unaffected, during sleeping and waking hours alike. Traveling is just one more a part of the whole picture. Chances are that it will be many years before your beach vacation will involve long hours of snoozing in the sun, daydreaming to the sound of the waves, and if that's what you have in mind, you'll be frustrated and disappointed.

With your young child, you'll be playing with the sand rather than lying on it and feeding the sea gulls rather than simply listening to them. You'll be kneeling and squatting more often than lying (learning about muscles you didn't know you had). You'll discover the small wonders of the earth—tiny seashells, shiny rocks, baby crabs, snails, crunchy dried seaweed, and such—following your child's cue.

Whether the glass is half full or half empty depends a lot on your outlook.

▶ Look forward to a trip like you've never had one before. Be ready to welcome such unexpected scenarios, and you're on your way.

- It's all in your attitude. Adventure is not so much a destination as it is a state of mind. And objectively, there's no such thing as a perfect vacation: Perfection is solely a matter of your perception.

- Opportunities lie in every situation that you might initially perceive as limiting.

- Take advantage of naps. They're a constant of life with young children; babies and many toddlers can't get through a day without them. But when your kids are snoozing, you and your partner can take turns being out and about—playing tennis, going shopping, reading a book by the pool. When they zone out on their bed, you can zone out on yours. You'll all be fresh enough to stay out a bit in the evening. You may even end the vacation feeling rested and relaxed, unlike the vast numbers of travelers who end their vacations needing a vacation to rest up.

- Set out on your journey with an open mind and a positive attitude, and whenever a situation looks as if it's going to get you down, be on the lookout for the silver lining. If you can see the humor in what's happening, give yourself a gold star.

Have a Guaranteed Place to Stay

Don't leave home without reservations. You don't want to be dealing with cranky, tired, and hungry babies or young children at the same time you're hunting for a room.

KTWF

<u>K</u>eep <u>T</u>hem <u>W</u>ell <u>F</u>ed. This goes without saying, but it's especially important when you're traveling. Hungry children have to eat—now—or everyone will share their unhappiness.

▶ If your room has a kitchenette or refrigerator and microwave, lay in supplies at the beginning of your stay and fix meals or snacks without going out.
▶ Travel with a supply of your youngster's favorite snacks.
▶ Plan on reaching restaurants before they fill up—be there at 11:30 AM for lunch, 5:30 PM for dinner— so your child has a chance to refuel before his tank is on empty.

Remember Routines

Because young kids thrive on the familiar, traveling can be stressful for them by its very nature. So provide as many constants as possible.

▶ Stick to your comfortable routines, adapting them as appropriate. For instance, although a baby's naptimes are sacred, nobody says you have to bed him down in your hotel room. You could also let him nap in the stroller while you pushed him through a quiet museum.
▶ Bring familiar items from home. Especially when traveling in other countries where flavors are

different, a jar of creamy peanut butter will go a long way toward making your youngster feel secure. His favorite teething biscuits or whatever you know will always do the trick.

▶ Pack your child's comfort object and to keep it readily accessible at all times—if it's buried in the trunk of your car or in the hold of the airplane, you'll be helpless.

▶ Bring extra pacifiers.

Stay Flexible

Adjustments have to be made when a whole family travels together. So, although you have to plan every trip as well as you can, you also have to stay alert to your child's signals on the road and be ready to go to Plan B or even Plan C if need be.

▶ Be prepared for the disruptions and changes when they occur. Say the daylong museum visit you've set your heart on proves to exceed your preschooler's endurance limit (and it probably will).

▶ Scale back your expectations (a one-hour stroll, anyone?).

Think Ahead

Adjusting to the bumps along your road is easier when you've anticipated them and scoped out strategies. By being resourceful, you can learn more about a place than many local residents will. Then it's just a matter of carefully picking and choosing. So do your homework.

- ▶ Find out as much about your destination in advance as you can.
- ▶ Use guidebooks, local newspapers, parents' magazines, and online resources such as family travel bulletin boards and discuss the options with people at your hotel.
- ▶ Buy a book of travel games and memorize a few that you think your youngster will like, so that you can introduce them as the need arises.

Be Creative

Use your head: Think about how your child will respond to periods of confinement, delays, and any other situations that may come up on the itinerary you've planned, and strategize accordingly.

For instance, instead of taking your sensitive daughter to a noisy, crowded state fair, look for a smaller event. Or spend your days pottering around a peaceful resort with a quiet lake beach. Before a cross-country airplane ride, you may want to do a few laps around the terminal with your favorite wiggleworm. The hundred-yard dash through London's National Gallery won't work? What about settling down for a few games of I Spy in front of just three or four major paintings? Is coaxing a toddler along as you trawl a flea market an uphill battle? You may manage an hour with a promise of a sojourn in a local pet store.

If you have ideas for responding to such situations, you'll be better prepared to come up with fun, creative ways to satisfy everyone's druthers.

Consider Baby-Sitting

No matter how intent you are on making your whole journey a family experience, a baby-sitter may well be part of the picture so that there's time for you and your spouse to be alone together. How much time you actually want to carve out is an individual matter but addressing the issue is essential in the planning stage of your trip because it will help you determine what kind of arrangements you need.

▶ Look for hotels that have on-site children's programs (though not all accept babies and young children still in diapers) or have baby-sitting services or a list of sitters.

▶ Ask friends, relatives, fellow employees, and business associates at home if they may know locals at your destination who may be able to provide a referral.

▶ Call the student employment office at local colleges and universities, churches and synagogues, seniors groups, or nursing schools for information about sitters.

▶ Bring your own sitter. A grandparent, teenage relative, neighbor, or your nanny enables you to take adult time frequently or helps during long intervals on your trip. Or travel with another family and split child care.

▶ Make any of arrangements that involve child care outside the hotel a week or two in advance.

Allow Plenty of Time

With small children, everything takes longer than you may expect and you'll only drive yourself crazy if you try to cut things too close.

One summer we took our toddler, Eric, to a family camp in the Sierras. We stayed in cabins with bathrooms and ate in a large dining hall with other young families. The experience was beautiful, relaxing, and outdoorsy without the inconveniences of tenting.

TRAVEL LOG

But the best part was that we traveled with another family and we traded baby-sitting duties. So one day my husband and I got to go sailing on the lake and another day we took a long hike alone. We also took our friends' two kids for long periods, so they had some quality time to themselves. At night, the four of us played cards together after the kids were in bed. The built-in baby-sitter idea worked out so well that before the trip was over, we were all discussing where we'd go together the next year.

—*Lindsay H., Walnut Creek, California*

- Start your planning and begin making lists as far ahead as you can.
- When the time comes to leave for the airport or think about lunch, don't wait until the last minute.
- Think of getting from place to place as part of the journey; don't wait until you arrive at your destination to start having fun. This is especially important if you're flying over the Christmas or Thanksgiving holidays.

Underplan

Discovering new things is one of the major pleasures of travel. But committing yourself to a jam-packed schedule from the outset won't allow you the time for such serendipities. Nor will it allow you to repeat favorite experiences as many children like to do—to go back to a restaurant they liked or revisit a playground or museum where they had a great time. So keep things loose.

DAILY ITINERARIES

As you plan out your travel days, include a generous dose of the activities your children love to do the most.

- Plan extra time for diaper changes, bathroom breaks, long naps, time to run around and play, and other downtime. Make sure that the activities you schedule not only allow enough time for such things but also places to do them. If your toddler usually naps at about four in the afternoon, be within striking distance of a good place for him to lie down by 3:45.

▶ Plan a variety of activities for each day rather than visiting every museum in a city park in one afternoon, even if it would be more convenient.

▶ Include a highlight for your child such as feeding pigeons or ducks in a park in each day's itinerary. If you plan to go out to eat, schedule in some time beforehand for him to run around somewhere. That

We found a week's worth of superb family activities in central San Diego last summer. Balboa Park has a great natural history museum. At the park's Reuben H. Fleet Space Theater, our preschooler, Thomas, loved the IMAX film on volcanoes and playing with the kid-friendly interactive exhibits in the lobby area. The park itself is huge, with great play areas for kids, and it's right next door to the San Diego Zoo.

TRAVEL LOG

—*Bonnie D., Bellingham, Washington*

way, he's more likely to be calmed down in the restaurant.

▶ Plan for alternative activities. If something goes amiss, you will know your options—other places you can visit that are nearby that might work better. For example, if your kids get bored and cranky while you're at a museum, you'll know where to find the nearest park, playground, or pet store, so you can head there next.

▶ Plan some open slots for your children to repeat activities they enjoy.

Getting the Most Out of Museums

If you go about it right, a museum trip can be just as thrilling to your kids as a day at the beach. Kids love to learn. Make the learning fun by sharing their experience.

Even for the youngest children, museums can work when chosen carefully. Babies may not understand what they're seeing in an art museum but enjoy bright colors. Many museums also have interactive exhibits. Those aimed at children are best, but even exhibits for general audiences entice young children to push the buttons and see what happens.

▶ Seek out smaller museums. Major museums can be so vast they intimidate children. Besides children's museums, more specialized museums such as historical, ethnic, crafts, aerospace, train and automobile museums are good options. If major museums are your only choice, target just one or two areas such as a good prehistoric exhibit at a natural history museum.

► Don't wear your kids out. Limit your visit to no more than two hours. If that isn't enough time to really take in the exhibits, you may be able to buy a pass that enables you to return a number of times over a several-day span.

► Stop in the gift store when you arrive and pick up postcards of the main attractions you're about to see. Your kids will probably love matching the real sights to the ones pictured on the cards.

► Don't overload your kids with information. As you make your way through the museum, point out a few things you think they'll appreciate most and then just allow them to soak up the atmosphere for themselves.

► Stop frequently to rest and snack to extend your stay. If you have packed your own juice and snacks you can easily feed your kids when they get hungry.

► Stop in the gift store on your way out to buy your kids a souvenir. This memento will help them remember the fun they had.

With babies

► If your baby gets fussy, take a break and walk outside. Baby may quiet down or even fall asleep.

► Check to see if strollers are available.

With toddlers and preschoolers

▶ If you've planned your museum visits in advance, get your kids interested in the subject matter before leaving home by reading related books to them.

▶ Increase your preschooler's interest in art exhibits by talking to him about the process of paintings, sculpture, and other forms of art you're viewing so he can imagine himself doing the same thing.

▶ Look for children's museums that teach kids about local culture. The museum in Portsmouth,

---

GOOD DINOSAUR MUSEUMS

☐ Las Vegas, Nevada, Natural History Museum

☐ Museum of the Rockies in Bozeman, Montana

☐ Sea World's Monster Marsh exhibit in Orlando, Florida

☐ American Museum of Natural History in New York City, New York

☐ New York State Museum in Albany, New York

☐ Museum of Western Colorado in Grand Junction, Colorado

☐ National Museum of Natural History in Washington, D.C.

New Hampshire, has a lobster boat complete with stormy-weather gear that kids can put on.

Finding the Best Parks and Playgrounds

No matter where in the world you plunk your family down, kids need time to relax and space to burn off excess energy. Being cooped up in cars, airplanes, and hotel rooms can take their toll. Just like at home, parks and playgrounds provide a pleasant play outlet. Finding the good ones can take some resourcefulness but you'll find it immensely satisfying when you score. And when you get back home, the skills you've learned on the road can help you find new family meccas in your own backyard.

- ▶ Ask the staff or other guests at the place you're staying to suggest parks, playgrounds, and other family attractions.
- ▶ Pick up brochures and maps in the hotel lobby or at a visitor center, which will show you the locations of various parks, playgrounds, and popular attractions and perhaps have descriptions.
- ▶ Check the listings in local newspapers.
- ▶ Ask friends, relatives, and work associates for contacts in the place you're visiting. They may know people you can call for suggestions. The best guidance often comes straight from local parents with similar needs.

Shop Smart

Although every area has its own distinctive flavor, shopping in the U.S. is getting more uniform every day, with large chain stores dominating local retail. Expect even modest-size cities to have shopping malls. While these may not have the most interesting local stores, the advantage for families is that they often have child care, so you can drop of your kids for awhile and shop at your leisure.

▶ When shopping with kids in tow, you'll often find benches to rest, food courts, and stands for diverse meal and snack choices, and enough commotion so that even cranky kids won't stand out in the crowd.

▶ Stop at places where your child can do some window shopping, such as at pet and toy stores, as long as you can resist his pleas to bring a brand new puppy back to the hotel room.

▶ Avoid places with small breakable items within easy reach, especially if your companions are grabby toddlers.

▶ Avoid places where the aisles are too narrow for easy maneuvering.

▶ Keep your child occupied. Bring a special toy for him that he gets to play with only on that occasion.

▶ If you're traveling with a partner, take turns staying with the kids and shopping.

Taming the Souvenir Monster

The young souvenir monster has a tendency to rear its head, especially when enticed by the endless variety of mementos he'll see during your travels. You can tame that souvenir monster by asking yourself the following questions when selecting souvenirs for your child.

▶ Is it practical? Hats, jackets, sweatshirts, T-shirts, sweaters, and so on will not only remind your child

---

TRAVEL LOG

My preschooler zeroed in on his favorite trading cards in a postcard shop in France last summer. We'd have normally rolled our eyes and resisted such a purchase, but when we discovered the cards were in French, we really couldn't hold out. Reading the familiar characters' names in the local language was fun for the whole family. And the cards were certainly easy enough to pack and bring home!

—*Christine C., Westport, Connecticut*

---

of your trip together but double as regular clothing when you return home.

▶ Is it educational? Postcards, pictures for kids' rooms, educational books about different places and cultures, and storybooks about people of other cultures teach your child about the places he has visited or will visit.

▶ Is it safe? Many countries have lower standards than the U.S. For example, some toys may be colored with lead paint. Dolls may have small parts that could detach and be swallowed. You are your own safety marshal when traveling. Inform yourself about common hazards in children's items and other consumer products by reading articles and books.

▶ How does it pack? Choose items that are soft and compact.

Theme Park Smarts

▶ Book a hotel that isn't too far from the site. Keep in mind that no matter how much fun your child has, he can wear out easily.

▶ Arrive at the park right after a nourishing breakfast and head for the most popular kiddy rides while your child is fresh and at peak excitement level. After a morning of activity, return to your hotel if you can for lunch and a break—either a quiet rest time for an hour or two, or some pool and beach time. Go back to the park for an early dinner, a few more attractions, and the evening's entertainment. This plan may give your child the balance of excitement and rest he needs to enjoy himself.

► Pay attention to the fear threshold. Even images and rides that seem innocent to you can scare your child. A four-year-old who is terrified of the first ride he experiences at Walt Disney World may be reluctant to experience any other attraction for the remainder of your stay. Start with the mildest rides and attractions and work your way up. Remember that sensations that seem mild to a grownup can feel much more powerful to a child; for a five-year-old the rapidly spinning teacups ride in the Disney parks could be way too wild.

► Purchase passes that can be used over several days instead of one-day tickets since your daily visits may be limited.

► Many parks with rides have what is unofficially known as "baby swap" areas, where two parents stand in line, one rides when their turn comes up while the other one holds the baby, and then the partner who waited takes her turn without an additional wait.

► If you do want to take your baby on some of the milder rides, avoid any ride that would jostle him.

ON THE WAY HOME

For toddlers and preschoolers especially, every minute you're on the road, return trip included, is part of your vacation. If you engage your children with this process, your children will have a much easier transition back to home life. Let them know in advance just how you will be getting home, what things you will do, and what sights you will see on the way. You just may be able to wring a little more fun out of your adventure together.

Children may get uneasy and anxious on the way home. Attention spans shorten and questions such as "Are we there yet?" or "When are we stopping?" may become more frequent.

▶ Talk to your kids about home, pets, friends, preschool, daycare, and other things that they miss from home.

▶ Review the places you've visited, sights you've seen, and encourage them to share their trip with their friends, daycare buddies, preschool classmates, baby-sitters, and grandparents.

▶ Do special things for/with your kids and remember that you're still on duty as entertainer and snack provider.

▶ Don't bring up things that might not have gone well while you were gone, such as a neighbor forgetting to feed the goldfish.

- Maintain your children's routines (bedtimes, story-times, mealtimes) as you did on the trip, getting as close to your kids' home schedules as possible, not only for them but also for you.

SAVOR THE MEMORIES

Savor vacation mode—at least for a day or two. Although the answering machine is blinking and the mail is piled to the sky, try to ease into your home routine gently.

- Give yourself and your child some time to decompress.
- Involve your child as you unpack.
- Help your child find a proper home for a cherished souvenir in your child's bedroom.
- Get your photographs developed right away, and plan a night to share them with your child.
- Make a memory book of postcards and/or photographs.
- Prepare a new food your child enjoyed on vacation at home just for fun.
- Speak often about favorite highlights of your vacation—and daydream together about where you want to go and what you want to do next year.

Appendix

Safety and Health

FLYING WITH A BABY

Before making your reservations, consider waiting until your baby is at least four weeks old before flying with her. In the first month of life, babies are extremely vulnerable to many viruses because their immune systems haven't developed defenses against them yet. Your child faces a higher-than-normal risk of catching a bug when flying because she's enclosed in a small space with a lot of people sharing the same recycled air for sometimes hours on end.

If you have travel plans that can't be rescheduled, you can fly with a healthy one-week-old. But avoid flying with a baby under four weeks old if she has a cold, cough, or ear infection. Check with your pediatrician before traveling if your baby is not completely healthy.

CHILD-PROOF ACCOMMODATIONS

▶ Childproof the room as soon as you arrive. Always pack outlet covers and drawer locks and put them to use as soon as possible. Put breakables, plastic bags, medicines, microwave oven, electrical cords, cleaning products, and other chemicals out of reach. Move wastebaskets off the floor and tie up any cords that dangle from shades or blinds.

▶ Protect your child from any falling furniture or heavy objects. Put all heavy or breakable items such as ashtrays and houseplants out of reach. Push table lamps away from furniture edges and secure wall units or bookcases to prevent them from crashing down on your child.

▶ Protect your child from dangerous places and situations. Make sure your accommodations have protective gates and put them in place as soon as you arrive. Check if the windows have either protective gates or locks out of your child's reach. Make sure the rails on a terrace or balcony are spaced closely

CHILD-PROOFING AWAY FROM HOME

Childproofing devices are compact and easily packed. The following items may not all be needed but you may want to bring them just in case:

- ☐ Electrical outlet covers
- ☐ Burner covers for kitchen facilities
- ☐ Faucet covers to prevent scalding accidents
- ☐ Bubble wrap for beveled glass tables and sharp corners on furniture
- ☐ Duct tape
- ☐ Cabinet and drawer locks
- ☐ Locks or string to keep your child from opening doors
- ☐ Baby gates

enough so a child can't fall through. Never leave your child alone on a terrace or balcony. If you stay in a ground-floor room, be sure that your child can't access a parking lot or swimming pool by herself. In any hotel or motel, be sure your child can't leave the room at night to wander in the hallways.

▶ Take a quick walk around your accommodations. Note any dangers not covered above and take care of them. When you go down to the pool, make sure the baby pool is safe for your child. Grates and drain covers should be secure and the pool bottom should not be slippery. Hotel pools and beaches rarely have lifeguards on duty, so never let your child out of your sight around water.

COMMON AILMENTS

Children face a higher risk of illness when you travel because their usual eating and sleeping routines get disrupted no matter how hard you try to avoid it. In addition, they may be stressed by the new experiences, hustling to make flights, and other rushing around. The following are the most likely medical problems your children will experience while you're on the road. In most cases, you can treat them the same way you would at home.

Colds

Colds are caused by viruses—not being cold or going out at night with wet hair. You can, however, take steps to keep children's colds to a minimum. Keep your child away from second-hand tobacco smoke as much as possible (a challenge in countries such as France and China). Limit exposure to other children, which may lessen exposure to cold viruses. This is not to say you have to keep your child in a germ-free box. If you have a variety of child-care options to choose from, those that put children in several small groups instead of one big one minimize exposure to cold viruses. Washing your and your child's hands helps prevent colds by not transmitting viruses.

Children's colds can be treated with one or two grams of Vitamin C per day spread out over the day. Have your child drink plenty of fluids, including chicken soup, which is effective in thinning cold-thickened mucus. Have her sip the soup slowly rather than drinking it down. Thick or crusty mucus from colds can also be treated with homemade saline nose drops (½ teaspoon of salt dissolved in 1 cup of lukewarm water). Treat one nostril at a time by putting one or two drops in the nostril. Allow the drops to work on the mucus for a minute or so. Then remove the thinned mucus with a bulb syringe. Repeat with the second nostril.

MEDICAL RECORDS

Remember to carry medical records and the phone number of your pediatrician (both for home and at your destination) in case of emergency.

Ear Infections

Although most ear infections heal on their own, it's best to treat them anyway to relieve your child's pain and because they sometimes lead to complications such as hearing loss. Appropriate drugs include acetaminophen (for pain relief) and antibiotics. When your child's in bed, elevate her head with a pillow. This will reduce pain by easing the pressure in her ear. Comfort your child with hugs, stories, and so on to help her feel better, in part because love and touching soothe and in part through sheer distraction.

Teething

Teething discomfort results from inflamed or swollen gums as the teeth break through. Although normal, the amount of pain varies widely from baby to baby. Irritability, drooling, chewing on objects, disturbed sleeping, and gum rubbing may all indicate teething pain. It can't be prevented but you can treat it by letting your baby chew on smooth, firm objects such as rings specifically designed for this purpose. Water-filled teething devices that can be cooled or ice wrapped in a cloth are other options. You can also try massaging baby's gums or using non-prescription gum-numbing medications.

Insect Bites and Stings

Most insect stings and bites have only minor effects unless the child is extremely allergic to them, which is extremely rare in young children. If you opt for a repellent, use only formulations labeled for infants or children. The American Academy of Pediatrics recommends one with no greater than 10 percent Deet (diethyl toluamide, the active ingredient used in popular children's brands). Wash the repellent off your child immediately when you come indoors to prevent ingestion or unnecessary absorption by the skin. A safe, natural alternative is oil of citronella. To help soothe itching from insect bites, sunburn, and rashes, apply a topical anti-itch medicine such as Calamine lotion.

MEDICAL SUPPLIES TO PACK

To ease your child's discomfort quickly and completely, pack a portable version of your medicine cabinet and include the following items:

▶ Antiseptic spray or antibiotic ointment. Apply to cuts and scrapes to prevent infection, then cover injury with bandage. Reapply when changing bandage. Do not use ointments after their expiration dates.

▶ Hydrogen peroxide or rubbing alcohol. Use for cleaning cuts and scrapes. Hydrogen peroxide is not quite as effective as rubbing alcohol but it's less painful for children.

▶ Liquid antihistamine. This does not fight colds but is sedating so may help an uncomfortable child sleep. Benadryl is a non-prescription example. Beware that some children have opposite reaction and become more active and irritable. Consult your physician before using.

- ▶ Acetaminophen. It provides safe, effective pain relief for headaches and other discomforts when used as recommended and brings down fever. Make sure you use infant- or child-strength as appropriate. Tylenol, Panadol, Tempra, St. Joseph's aspirin-free, Anacin-3, Liquiprin are all non-prescription examples. It's available in drops, liquid, tablets, or suppositories.

- ▶ Ibuprofen. Like acetaminophen, this provides relief for headaches and other discomforts, but lasts about two hours longer. Although it's safe when used as recommended, it may cause stomach upset. Ibuprofen and other naproxen-containing products can also trigger asthma attacks. Non-prescription examples include Advil and Nuprin.

- ▶ Syrup of ipecac. For inducing vomiting in case of poisoning. Call physician or poison center before using.

- ▶ Activated charcoal. For absorption of caustic poison that has been ingested.

- ▶ Rehydration fluid/electrolyte solution. Sold under brand names such as Pedialyte, Lytren, Ricelyte, or Resol. Use to treat dehydration from overheating or after prolonged vomiting or diarrhea.

- ▶ Thermometer. Use rectal, ThermoScan digital, or other child-safe type.

- ▶ Nasal bulb syringe. For clearing stuffy nostrils when child is too young to blow her nose.

- ▶ Calibrated medicine dropper or spoon. Looks like test tube with spoon attached. Allows you to deliver a measured amount of medicine without spilling. Use bulb syringe for babies.

▶ Tweezers. Angle-edged are the most versatile because they have both points and flat surfaces.

▶ Variety of bandage materials. Adhesive tape, sterile gauze pads, elastic bandages, and adhesive bandages. You can also use the pads to apply antibiotic ointment or antiseptic. Remove adhesive tape in one quick movement to minimize discomfort.

▶ Clean, sharp pair of scissors. For cutting bandaging materials.

▶ Sunscreen. Use only preparations specially formulated for babies and children. Choose waterproof, broad-spectrum type with SPF (sun protection factor) 15 or higher. Test for allergic reaction first by putting a small amount on your child's wrist. Apply 30 minutes before sun exposure and reapply frequently as directed on bottle.

MOTION SICKNESS

If your child experiences nausea from motion sickness, try non-drug methods first. Open a window and have her sit facing forward and look at something that is not moving, such as the horizon. To prevent motion sickness, travel when your child sleeps, keep her away from second-hand smoke, and don't let her stare at books in the car.

Herbal alternatives also help ease or prevent nausea caused by motion sickness. Ginger ale and tea are popular remedies. Other herbal tea alternatives include chamomile and peppermint. Natural foods stores and supermarkets may carry herbal blends recommended for stomach upsets. Some people prefer motion sickness wrist bands, which have a small plastic bead on the inside that puts pressure on acupressure points on the wrist. You can buy these over the counter at many pharmacies under such brands as Bioband.

Ask your pediatrician about the following medications for motion sickness in young children:

▶ Benadryl (diphenhydramine). Makes most children drowsy as well as thirsty. Will make some children more active and irritable.
▶ Dramamine (dimenhydrinate). Chemically similar to Benadryl with similar effects. Do not give to children under two.
▶ Tigan (trimethobenzamide). Prescription anti-nausea medication chemically similar to Benadryl and Dramamine. Tigan is only prescribed for children two and older.
▶ Pepto-Bismol. Helps soothe upset stomach. Do not give to a child with flu or chicken pox because of risk of Reye's syndrome.

- ▶ Phenergan (promethazine). Prescription anti-nausea medication that helps prevent motion sickness. Highly sedating.
- ▶ Compazine (prochloroperazine). Prescription drug that is chemically similar to Phenergan.

AN EMERGENCY MEDICAL GUIDE

Medical professionals are the best people to handle crisis situations. If you find yourself in an emergency, get a doctor. Here are some common travel-related medical situations and what you can do about them.

Food Poisoning

Eating at restaurants and food stands always increases the chances of food poisoning, whether you're in your hometown or on the other side of the world. Most food poisoning is not serious and can be treated without seeing a doctor. General symptoms include nausea, abdominal cramps, vomiting, diarrhea, and fever. Bacteria cause all food poisoning no matter which food is involved.

Call the doctor if you notice unusual weakness, tingling, numbness, or mental/behavioral signs such as confusion, hallucinations, or agitation or the above signs of botulism poisoning. If your child is dehydrated, use a rehydration solution such as Pedialyte to replace electrolytes.

Return your child to her normal diet gradually and only after she tells you she is hungry. Start with simple foods such as clear soups and progress to starchy foods such as bananas, plain toast, noodles, rice cereal, and potatoes as she begins to feel better. Breastfeeding or feeding with formula can be continued throughout.

DEHYDRATION

If your baby has been vomiting or has had diarrhea for three or more hours, check for dehydration. Try this simple test: Gently pull a fold of your baby's skin with your thumb and forefinger and let it go. It should fall back in place immediately. If it stays tented for a bit then slowly returns to shape, the tissues have lost too much water and you should consult with a doctor.

Types of food poisoning

Below are the types of food poisoning and their related causes and symptoms:

▶ Staphylococcus aureus. This is the most common variety. It is usually transmitted from an infected person's hands. The symptoms first appear about six hours after eating and are gone after about a day.

▶ Salmonella. These bacteria are found in some raw meat, eggs, and unpasteurized milk. The symptoms appear about 16–48 hours after eating and last two to seven days.

▶ Botulism. This is the most serious form of food poisoning. Although it's extremely rare, it can be life-threatening. It is likely to come from improperly canned foods with low acid content, such as corn, beets, and string beans. Children under a year can also get botulism from honey. The symptoms differ from other forms of food poisoning. They include headache, muscle paralysis, vomiting, double vision, difficulty breathing and swallowing, extreme weakness, numbness, and tingling. In babies, the symptoms are constipation, lethargy, and poor muscle tone. Symptoms appear 18–36 hours after eating and can last for months.

Food poisoning prevention

The following tips will help you prevent food poisoning:

▶ Never prepare food if you're suffering from food poisoning-like symptoms yourself.

▶ Wash your hands thoroughly before all food preparation.

- ▶ Buy meat and seafood only from sources you trust. If none are available, a vegetarian diet is perfectly safe for you and your child with some minor precautions. Keep in mind many vegetarian foods are low in fat and protein. Children under two may need extra fat and children under seven may need extra protein. Pregnant and lactating moms also need extra protein. Good vegetarian protein sources include soy products, dairy products, eggs, legumes (lentils, beans, peanuts), nuts, and seeds.
- ▶ When preparing raw meat including chicken and seafood, wash your hands afterward and wash both utensils and cutting board with warm soap and water before using them for other foods.
- ▶ Cook all meat thoroughly. Be aware, however, that although this will kill salmonella bacteria, it will not prevent staphylococcus aureus poisoning. Toxins produced by the bacteria, not the bacteria themselves, cause the latter.
- ▶ Wash your hands after using the bathroom or changing a diaper.
- ▶ Throw out canned foods if the liquid is milky, the container is cracked or unsealed in any way, the lid is loose, or the can is bulging.
- ▶ Never feed honey to children younger than one year old.
- ▶ Don't allow foods to sit at room temperature for more than two hours.

- Reheat cooked foods thoroughly.
- Keep refrigerated foods cold.
- Avoid raw eggs and throw out those that are cracked. Cook eggs for at least three minutes.
- Avoid raw milk and raw meats of all types.
- Avoid foods that smell or taste strange or spoiled, even in clean restaurants.
- Avoid foods that spoil or become easily contaminated such as mayonnaise and dairy products in less-developed countries.

Ear Pain while Flying

Shifts in cabin pressure during take-off, landing, and other altitude changes can make children's ears hurt.

With babies

Babies are particularly vulnerable to ear pain because of their tiny Eustachian tubes. Breast feeding during take-off and landing prevents ear pain. Alternatives are sucking on bottle or a pacifier.

With toddlers and preschoolers

Vigorously chewing gum helps to relieve pressure. Try placing warm, moist washcloths over your child's ears. If you've flown with your child before and know she's prone to ear problems, fly non-stop to minimize her discomfort.

All young children

Congestion can contribute to ear discomfort. If your child is stuffed-up, talk to your pediatrician before the flight. An antihistamine may be required.

Altitude Sickness

Mild headache and nausea can be treated with children's acetaminophen. Prevent dehydration by having your child drink plenty of water (soda, milk, and juice are not substitutes). Dehydration can contribute to symptoms.

Sunburn

The tender skin of children is highly susceptible to the sun's rays. They can get sunburned in any season and even on cloudy or hazy days. Keep skin hydrated and

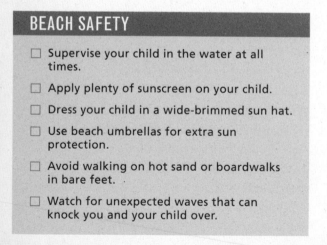

BEACH SAFETY

- ☐ Supervise your child in the water at all times.
- ☐ Apply plenty of sunscreen on your child.
- ☐ Dress your child in a wide-brimmed sun hat.
- ☐ Use beach umbrellas for extra sun protection.
- ☐ Avoid walking on hot sand or boardwalks in bare feet.
- ☐ Watch for unexpected waves that can knock you and your child over.

cool with aloe-vera lotion. Apply damp washcloths to reduce the pain.

You can prevent sunburn with sunscreen and by putting a wide-brimmed hat or a bonnet on your child and provide shade protection at the beach and in the stroller. Keep infants out of direct sunlight, especially during the peak sun hours of 10 AM to 2 PM. Start off toddlers and preschoolers with short exposures in summer and increase the time gradually as their skin adjusts to the sun.

Prickly Heat

Prickly heat is an itchy, irritating rash that infants are particularly susceptible to in hot weather. It occurs when sweat becomes trapped in the baby's undeveloped pores. Prickly heat appears as tiny pink bumps on a red base, generally along the scalp line, the scalp itself, and around the ears, neck, chest, and back. The bumps may be full of clear fluid.

Dress your baby in loose-fitting cotton clothing after bathing to help prevent prickly heat. She should drink plenty of water; keep her indoors if possible.

If your baby has prickly heat, immediately take her to a cooler place to keep the condition from worsening. The discomfort eventually disappears but can be eased with a cool Colloidal oatmeal bath.

Heat Exhaustion

Heat exhaustion occurs when the body's cooling system overworks itself because of excessive heat exposure. On hot days, keep your child hydrated with plenty of water. Stay away from caffeinated sodas, which are diuretic and will dehydrate her. Don't let your child overexert herself when it's very hot. If your child develops headache, stupor, dizziness, or weakness, or has pale, clammy skin, get her out of the heat immediately and into the shade or a cool room. Have her drink plenty of water. Call a physician immediately if she refuses to drink or can't keep water down.

HIKING SAFETY

With babies: Avoid hiking in any extremes of heat, cold, dampness, or wind. Limit sun exposure, apply sunscreen frequently, give your baby extra juice or water, and take frequent rest breaks. Even babies who are carried by a parent need to get out of the carrier and stretch occasionally. At high altitudes, especially, your child will be exposed to intense sun rays, need more fluids, and tire more quickly. Consult with your physician before going if your baby has a medical condition, such as an infection.

With baby in a pack, your safety and hers are one and the same. Look for smooth trails, avoid rock scrambles, and wear footgear that grips firmly.

Take your time and watch out for obstacles that could cause falls. Carry a lightweight mirror, so you can check over your shoulder to see how your baby is doing while you're hiking.

With toddlers and preschoolers: Avoid trails bordering rapid streams or lakes that might tempt your toddler. Dress her in layers that protect her from the weather, and tuck long pants into socks to protect her from insect bites and poison ivy. Take lots of short breaks so she won't get tired or bored, and carry plenty of drinks and snacks so her hunger or thirst doesn't cut short your excursion.

INTERNATIONAL HEALTH AND SAFETY ISSUES

International travel can be hard on bodies, big or small, because you're exposed to unfamiliar foods, water, climate, altitudes, and environmental hazards. In addition, your family's immune systems may not be prepared for local diseases. This holds true even in modern, developed countries. Plus, the emotional stress of dealing with different languages and customs can also compromise your immunity.

To receive regular updates about worldwide health risks, join the International Association for Medical

Assistance to Travelers (IAMAT), a non-profit foundation established in 1960 that advises travelers about health risks, international climate conditions, geographical distribution of diseases, sanitation conditions in different countries, and immunization requirements for most countries. IAMAT will also provide names of competent Western-trained, English-speaking physicians as well as locations of hospitals in 450 cities and 200 countries (see Family Resources section).

Health Advisories in Foreign Countries

The Centers for Disease Control and Prevention (CDC) in the United States maintains up-to-date information about disease outbreaks worldwide and the best protections from them (see Family Resources section). Check with them no later than six weeks before you travel.

Immunizations

Routine childhood immunizations should be up to date or even accelerated prior to international travel. The Centers for Disease Control and Prevention (CDC) has current information on recommended and necessary vaccinations for adults and children traveling abroad. Find out what's required for travel to specific destinations. In addition, the CDC recommends that you review the following vaccines with your pediatrician as far in advance of travel as possible to ensure the proper scheduling of recommended vaccines:

- Diphtheria, tetanus, and acellular pertussis (DtaP)
- Measles, mumps, and rubella (MMR)
- Polio vaccine (IPV)
- Hepatitis B
- Haemophilus influenzae type b (Hib)
- Varicella vaccine

Keep in mind that some immunizations must be received four to six weeks to provide full protection. Others must be taken as a series of shots over time. Some medications

IMMUNIZATION CHECKLIST FOR FOREIGN TRAVEL

- ☐ Check with your physician or Centers for Disease Control and Prevention (CDC) about immunization requirements and recommended boosters and medications to pack.

- ☐ Get immunizations four to six weeks prior to departure.

- ☐ Allow time for immunizations that require a series of shots for full immunity.

- ☐ Pack sufficient medication for your trip and whatever information you need to take the medication correctly.

- ☐ At least six weeks before you depart, contact the CDC about disease outbreaks in the areas you are traveling to and special precautions you should take to protect your family from them.

must be taken before, during, and after travel for protection from disease. Be sure to plan ahead.

Medication Equivalents in Foreign Countries

Knowing the medication names for the drug brands you use at home is essential when traveling abroad. The same drug may be sold under a different brand name in another country, and you can buy the drug as a generic (non-brand name version if you know the medication name). To prevent communication difficulties with a foreign pharmacist, write the medication name and the strength you want on a slip of paper.

COMMON MEDICATION NAMES

The following medications include the medication name and its brand name in parentheses:

▶ **Antibiotic cream or ointment: clindamycin (Cleocin), erythromycin; meclocycline (Meclan); tetracycline**

▶ **Antihistamines: brompheniramine (Dimetane), chlorpheniramine maleate (Chlortrimeton), clemastine fumarate (Tavist), dyphenhdramine (Benadryl), triprolidine (Actidil)—all non-prescription; cyproheptadine (Periactin) and hydroxyzine (Atarax)—both prescription**

▶ **Anti-itch: cortisone, prescription**

- ▶ Anti-nausea: dimenhydrinate (Dramamine)— non-prescription; prochloroperazine (Copazine), promethazine (Phenergan), trimethobenzamide (Tigan)—all prescription
- ▶ Pain and fever relief: acetaminophen (Tylenol, Panadol, Tempra, St. Joseph's aspirin-free, Anacin-3, Liquiprin); ibuprofen (Advil, Nuprin)

Family Resources

Fodor's Resources

Guidebooks

Family Adventure Vacations

Profiles different types of soft adventures, discussing what each is like with kids of different ages, from infants on up, and recommends outfitters and trips. Each suggested trip comes with age-appropriateness rating.

Fodor's Around the City with Kids

A series of small, lively guides that map out great days together in the cities they cover, with volumes covering Boston, Chicago, Los Angeles, Miami, New York, San Francisco, Washington, D.C., London, Paris, and Toronto. All the authors are local parents, and every site comes with an age-appropriateness rating, from infant through age 16.

Fodor's Gold Guides

Every one of the more than 100 guides in Fodor's flagship series includes information about availability of American and local brands of diapers, formula, and other necessities of the pre-school years, as well as great tips on family-friendly *hotels and sights that kids like.*

Fodor's Road Guide USA

A 15-volume series jam-packed with places your family can stay, eat, and play in thousands of communities, from big cities to small towns, all across the USA.

On the Web

fodors.com

The Family Travel Center page includes kids travel tips, information about favorite family destinations, smart travel tips, family travel columns, news, features, and more. You can also post specific questions and get answers from fellow travelers who have been there with their own youngsters.

Air Travel

Federal Aviation Administration (FAA)

800/FAA-SURE (322-7873)
faa.gov/apa/apahome.htm
For information on using car seats when flying.

Car Rental Agencies

Avis Rental Car
800/230-4898
avis.com

Budget Rental Car
800/527-0700
drivebudget.com

Dollar Rental Car
800/800-3665
dollar.com

Hertz Rental Car
800/654-9998
hertz.com

Thrifty Car Rental
800/847-4309
thrifty.com

Auto Europe
800/223-5555
autoeurope.com
Also has information on hotels and discounted airfares.

Family-Friendly All-Inclusives

Club Med
75 Valencia Avenue
Coral Gables, FL 33134
clubmed.com
800/CLUB MED

Family-Friendly Cruise Lines

American Hawaii Cruises
800/543-7637
cruisehawaii.com

Carnival
800/327-9501
carnival.com

Disney
800/939-2784
disneycruise.com

Holland America
800/426-0327
hollandamerica.com

Norwegian Cruise Line
800/327-7030
ncl.com

Princess Cruises
800/774-6237
princesscruises.com

Royal Caribbean International
800/827-6400
rccl.com

Family-Friendly Hotels

Best Western
bestwestern.com
800/780-7234

Days Inn
daysinn.com
800/544-8313

DoubleTree Hotel
doubletree.com
800/222-TREE

Four Seasons Hotels and Resorts
fourseasons.com
800/819-5053

Holiday Inn
holiday-inn.com
800/465-4329

Howard Johnson
hojo.com
800/406-1411

Hyatt Hotels
hyatt.com
800/633-7313

Marriott Hotels
marriott.com
800/932-2198

Ramada Hotels
ramada.com
888/298-2054

Sheraton Hotels and Resorts
sheraton.com
888/625-5144

Family-Friendly Travel Agencies

Backroads
801 Cedar Street
Berkeley, CA 94710
800/462-2848
backroads.com
Family biking trips in the US; walking tours in Canada, Hawaii, and Washington.

Family Travel Connection
Family Cruise Specialists
Safety Harbor, FL 34695
888/799-2336
familytravelconnection.com
Represents all of the major cruise lines.

Familyworld Tours
16000 Ventura Boulevard, Suite 200
Encino, CA 91436
818/990-6777
International tours for parents traveling with children ages four months and up.

Grand Travel
6900 Wisconsin Avenue, Suite 706
Chevy Chase, MD 20815
800/247-7651
301/986-0790
grandtrvl.com
Specializing in trips for grandparents and grandchildren.

Kids Go Too
Box 3478
Winter Park, CO 80482
800/638-3215
kidsgotootravel.com
Family packages for vacations in the Rocky Mountains.

Personal Touch Travel
65 Rombout Road
Poughkeepsie, NY 12603
877/485-7221
debgio-ctc.com
Excursions all over the world.

Rascals in Paradise

Family Travel Specialists
650 Fifth Street, Suite 505
San Francisco, CA 94107
800/U-RASCAL
415/978-9800
415/442-0289 Fax
rascalsinparadise.com
Packages include baby-sitters, special kids menus, separate mealtimes for children, and organized activities.

Sealed with a Kiss

Box 2063
Rockville, MD 20847
800/888-7925
eswak.com
Custom-made travel packages

Family-Friendly Web Sites

Air Travel with Multiples

owc.net/~twins/flying.htm
Arranges flights, seating, car seats, and strollers; information on packing and in-flight issues.

American Academy of Pediatrics

aap.org
Excellent tips for keeping your kids safe from the sun.

BabyCenter.com

babycenter.com
Sells travel supplies; helps plan a safe trip.

Baby Travel Solutions

BabyTravelSolutions.com
Sells diapers, food, wipes and infant toiletries for delivery directly to your hotel room.

Evenflo

evenflo.com
Sells car seats, strollers, and other baby care products; provides safety information, consumer services, and helpful links.

Family Go

family.go.com
Search engine with articles about kid-friendly trips.

Family Travel Forum

familytravelforum.com
Travel specialists with airfare restaurant reviews, information about specific destinations, and helpful links.

Family Web

familyweb.com
Childproofing and other travel tips.

Home Hardware Dealers

homehardwaredealers.com
Games for the road and plane packing lists.

Tiny Travelers

tinytravelers.net
Articles about traveling with infants and infant products.

Travel with Kids

travelwithkids.com
State-by-state guide for family attractions around the country, many articles.

Gear

eBags

800/820-6126
eBags.com
Sells durable luggage.

Magellan's

800/962-4943
magellans.com
Sells items from jet-lag prevention medicine to outdoor wear.

Sharper Image

800/344-5555
sharperimage.com
Sells high-end products, from luggage to alarm clocks.

Travelsmith

800/950-1600
travelsmith.com
Sells quality travel gear and clothing.

Home Rentals and Exchanges

CyberRentals

CyberRentals.com
Exclusively devoted to rental listings.

Dejanews

DejaNews.com
Locate rentals and exchanges by posting notices to online newsgroups, forums, or boards.

Home Exchange

homeexchange.com
Budget home rentals within the U.S.

Holi-Swaps

holi-swaps.com
Rent, trade, or exchange your home and take your family anywhere in the world.

Home Base Holidays

homebase-hols.com

Cheap travel and comfortable accommodations all around the world.

International Home Exchange Network

homexchange.com

For home exchanges and some rental listings.

Mountain Lodging

mountain-lodging.com

Mountain lodgings from inns to bungalows, all across the US and parts of Canada.

Vacation Home Rentals

vacationhomerentals.com

An assortment of family homes from beach houses to mountain cottages across North America.

Web Home Exchange

webhomeexchange.com

Worldwide affordable homes.

International Travel

Non-Medical Information

American Automobile Association (AAA)
1000 AAA Drive
Heathrow, FL 32745-5063.
Authorized by U.S. State Department to issue online International Driving Permit applications.

American Automobile Touring Alliance (AATA)

1151 E. Hillsdale Blvd.
Foster City, CA 94404
800/622-7070
Fax: 650/294-7105
Alternate contact for International Driving Permits authorized by U.S. State Department.

Federal Consumer Information Center

pueblo.gsa.gov

Information on entry requirements to various countries, including passport requirements.

U.S. Department of State

900/225-5674 or 888/362-8668.
travel.state.gov

For passports and information regarding road security abroad. The 900 number is a toll call. The 888 number is toll-free but you will need a credit card. Download DSP-11 passport application from Web site. A live operator can tell you the status of your application (for a fee).

Medical Information

International Association for Medical Assistance to Travelers

417 Center Street
Lewiston, NY 14092
716/754-4883
sentex.net/iamat

Centers for Disease Control and Prevention

1600 Clifton Road
Atlanta, GA 30333
General information:
800/311-3435
Travelers information:
877/394-8747
cdc.gov

Foreign and Commonwealth Office

fco.gov.uk

Medical Advisory Services for Travelers Abroad (MASTA)

masta.org

World Health Organization

525 23rd Street, NW
Washington, DC 20037
202-861-3200
who.int

Products

Babies "R" Us

888/222-9787
babiesrus.com

Baby Trend

800/328-7363
babytrend.com

Evenflo
800/233-5921
evenflo.com

Fisher-Price
800/828-4000
fisher-price.com

Gerber
800/443-7237
gerber.com

Jack Rabbit Creations
404/876-4225
jackrabbitcreations.com

Kolcraft
800/453-7673
kolcraft.com

Osh Kosh B'Gosh
800/282-4674
oshkoshbgosh.com

Smarter Kids
800/293-9314
smarterkids.com

Toys "R" Us
888/243-6337
toysrus.com

Train Travel

Brit Rail
888/BRITRAIL
britrail.com

Rail Europe
800/4EURAIL
raileurope.com

Weather

Lowe's Storm 2000
gopbi.com/weather/storm/

National Hurricane Center
nationalhurricanecenter.com

National Oceanic and Atmospheric Administration (NOAA)
14th Street & Constitution Avenue, NW
Room 6013
Washington. DC 20230
202/482-6090
noaa.com

National Weather Service, NOAA
1325 East-West Highway
Silver Spring, MD 20910
nationalweatherservice.com

Tropical Prediction Center
11691 S.W Prediction Center
Miami, Florida 33165-2149
305/229-4470
nhc.noaa.gov

Fodor's
Key to the Guides

America's guidebook leader publishes guides for every kind of traveler—check out our many series and find your perfect match.

Fodor's Gold Guides

America's best-selling travel guide series offers the most detailed insider reviews of hotels, restaurants, and attractions in all price ranges, plus great background information, smart tips, useful maps, and more.

Fodor's Road Guide USA

Big guides for a big country—the most comprehensive guides to America's roads, packed with places to stay, eat, and play across the USA. Just right for road warriors, family vacationers, cross-country trekkers, and anyone hitting the road.

COMPASS AMERICAN GUIDES

Stunning guides from top local writers and photographers—gorgeous photos, literary excerpts, colorful anecdotes, and more. A must-have for culture mavens, history buffs, and new residents.

Fodor's CITYPACKS

Concise city coverage with a fold-out map. The right choice for urban travelers who want everything under one cover.

Fodor's EXPLORING GUIDES

Hundreds of color photos bring your destination to life; lively stories share insight into the culture, history, and people. Great for independent explorers who want in-depth background coverage.

ADDITIONAL GUIDES →

Fodor's POCKET GUIDES
For travelers who don't need as much information—the best of
Fodor's in pocket-size packages for just $10.

Fodor's To Go
Credit-card sized, magnetic color microguides that fit right in the
palm of your hand—perfect for "stealth" travelers or as gifts.

Fodor's FLASHMAPS
Every resident's map guide: 60 easy-to-follow maps: public transit,
parks, museums, zip codes, and more.

Fodor's CITYGUIDES
Sourcebooks for living in the city: Thousands of in-the-know listings
for restaurants, shops, sports, nightlife, and other city resources.

Fodor's AROUND THE CITY WITH KIDS
Great ideas for family days in your own backyard or on the road.

Fodor's upCLOSE
Travel well, spend less with these lively guides for travelers who
crave value and want to get away from the crowds.

Fodor's ESCAPE
Fill your trip with once-in-a-lifetime experiences, from ballooning in
Chianti to overnighting in the Moroccan desert. These full-color
dream books point the way.

Fodor's Languages for Travelers
Learn the local language before hitting the road. Available in
Phrase Books or Audio Sets.

Karen Brown's Guides
Engaging guides to the most charming inns and B&Bs in the USA
and Europe, with easy-to-follow inn-to-inn itineraries.

Baedeker's Guides
Comprehensive guides trusted since 1829, packed with A–Z reviews and star ratings.

Fodor's Around the City with Kids guides
make it easy to plan great family days.

★ The inside scoop on fun spots
  all over the city

★ Insider tips and way-cool trivia

★ Kid-friendly snack spots

★ Age-appropriateness ratings

---

*"You'll love the activity recommendations and kid-friendly eats.
Children will love the moving flip art." —Family Life*